Autistic Brothers
and Bipolar me.

"A frank and brutally honest diary from a mother with Bipolar and her two Autistic boys"

By E J Plows

For Harry and Gran.

Acknowledgements.

First and foremost I have to thank Jon. He has always supported me in everything I have ever wanted to do know matter how silly or crazy. I tell him over and over that he came into my life at the age of Seventeen to save me.

My children, they will never understand the strength, courage and sheer determination they have transformed my immature, vain shell into. They made me fight when I needed to and be calm when they needed me to be.

My grandparents are the ones I go to when I have good news and bad news, when I need a cuddle or just a gossip. The love I have for them I can't describe.

Jo Jo. For been as barmy as me on occasion and been a true friend when I was so ill in the early days. I'm here whenever you need the favour returning.

Last but not least. Mum, thank you, for been the only one who ever believed me when I needed help for Noah, x.

Autistic blessings and Bipolar Me.

Many, many people in my life have and still do to this day blurt out the phrase "God I feel sorry for you, it must be hard being you! How do you cope?" I generally smile, sometimes I reply that I'm actually really lucky and would rather have my life than theirs any day. I know that's rude, but the misconceptions of having Bipolar and two Autistic children really irritates me. Noah has Asperger's syndrome and has a routine and after a while is quite easy to get to know. Moses is harder to cope with; I find it hard to understand him. I long for the day that my son says I love you mummy and be really proud of who he is.

In February 2007 I was diagnosed with Bipolar type one after a long battle with post natal depression, where I was hospitalised numerous times. Throughout the period between 2004 to 2009 myself Noah and Moses were all given a diagnosis of something life changing, but as a mother I refuse to be labelled and judged by a medical condition. I am Emma Plows I am not Emma Plows with Bipolar.

It's my understanding that when you discover your child is on the autistic spectrum you really need to accept the diagnosis. Accept it, let it grow and don't hinder its development. Autistic people cannot understand how the world works like we can and have difficulty understanding how people think, but we can. We have that capacity to understand them, if we choose too we should take advantage of that capacity. If we don't accept that our children are autistic, then we are only condemning ourselves and our children to a life of frustrating misery. Work with it, not against it, it doesn't matter why they behave the way they do as we cannot change it, but we must find the beauty in the condition and all the positives it has to offer, if we try, it gets easier and can become very rewarding.

A year in the life of a confused and not so nuclear family.

Monday. The screams get to me but I try to somehow become immune by just riding it out and accepting it. Because that's all I can do, accept it. I have a little machine up there in his bedroom, locked in a speeded up world that doesn't have a malfunction but just manifests and communicates itself in a different way to every other blonde little cheeky boy. Moses is a very clever lad; I'm not just saying that because he's my son. But rather that he's old before his time and when we talk it's like I'm talking to a rather sophisticated adult. Be it one who has an attitude problem and clever wit.

Tuesday. Noah is in his final year of primary school. The school is situated on our rather nice, almost middle class estate nestled amongst the pink blossom trees with motherly cliques collecting their little darlings. Today I had the last meeting for Noah before his transition to high school. Ever since his diagnosis at the age of four, high school has been my main worry for his future. In the meeting all the people who have had some relation to Noah in his school life were there. Each gave their input and believed it to be utterly valid and vital to his cause. These meeting are important and this one none more so, but it generally ends up with nine or ten women talking over each other. They contradict, correct and argue... Politely. I must admit I am not always as polite as them, I suppose I am more passionate about my cause than them? But one thing I have learned throughout this whole process is you cannot Lose it!...... Keep your cool because as soon as you lose your composure people stop listening and stop taking you seriously. Believe me it's hard enough to have your small voice heard as it is.

Wednesday.
I feel positive today. After a very reluctant two years of being convinced by my psychiatrist that I really need to be on Lithium for my Bipolar, I finally succumbed and started the meds. I have been taking them now for five weeks and I'm starting to feel much more levelled out. I still have a temper and I feel like I'm losing my mind and my brain has turned to shit but all in all I'm feeling more hopeful.

The meeting yesterday actually went really well. The bonus of the whole meeting was that while I was there and speaking to the woman from the Education authority, I was handed a brown envelope. Inside was Moses's statement. Finally after a year of letters, tribunal forms, parent groups and numerous phone calls we got it. I had tears in my eyes and I think she did too. I couldn't believe that after a year I had finally got it. I knew it was just a matter of time and me not giving up. It's all about money and it makes me sick. The Education authority is a huge organisation, full of small subsidiary groups. These groups come to your home and show you how to start the tribunal process. What they also tell you is that you will never get to the tier 2 part of the tribunal because it costs them thousands of pounds. So they'll drop it. But no, it can't be about money. My arse!

Anyway, it's been made rather clear during the meeting that all Noah's special needs will be met and we had a very in-depth conversation about his support and safety at high school. I felt at ease after the meeting, usually I just get bloody wound up by the bunch of nonsensical mutterers waiting for their turn to talk. I went home and tried to hug Moses, but he was on the Wii, so I hugged Ben instead and gave him a little smile. Today was a good day.

Thursday.

I had to go to the doctors today because I keep getting really bad headaches and need something stronger for them. When I went in, it wasn't my usual doctor. I told the doctor about my migraines and she told me it was depression. Right, so you've asked me nothing about the way I feel, nothing about what's happening in my life and nothing about stress. You see the thing is unless you have a good relationship with your regular doctor any doctor will put a broken finger, constipation, decapitation or leaking nipples down to the fact that you have bipolar. I once had a temperature of 104 and aches and pains for three weeks my husband had literally carried me in and the doctor said depression. I went home and had a fit on the living room floor. I was in hospital for three weeks with glandular fever. One of the best attributes to being a doctor is listen more than you speak!

Friday.

Right, I am sick to my stomach today. I'm going to have to interact with friends and get organised. A lot is happening and although it's all good stuff its change. I hate change. It's my birthday party tomorrow, although I am not the birthday girl until Monday. I do this every year where it's all about me! But this year

I'm sharing it with my friend Anita who is nowhere near as organised as me and as much as I love her, she drives me mad.

Nerves.

Saturday.
I can't talk to anyone about anything other than my party because I have to focus. I'm really not coping but I'll take it hour by hour; hold Ben's hand and think, all about me, all about me, all about me.

Sunday.
It was brilliant. It was a fancy dress party in a cocktail bar in the town centre. I was Daphne from Scooby doo but I don't think anyone noticed. In all honesty I don't remember that much because as I don't generally drink I got drunk rather quickly. I remember dancing, drinking fifteen shots, one pitcher and four beers. Oh and a mini cone of fish and chips. After two hours I had to go, I didn't say goodbye to anyone, got in a taxi, got out, sat on the toilet and vomited in the sink. I wasn't proud of myself but I think I had fun, the pictures say I did anyway.

I've been thinking. Don't we as mothers put so much pressure on ourselves? How much is too long on the Wii? How long on after school activities? Does he have enough friends? Is his grammar as good as the other kids? Women, and men, but mostly women have and put far too much pressure on themselves to be super mum. Why? Yes we want our little gilberts to do well but when you have children with autism, handicapped of disabled, all you want is happiness for them. What more should a mother really want?

A bad week.

Monday. Today Ben and I had a psychiatrist appointment luckily without Moses because I lost it, "Just put him on medication". I hate my son I fucking hate my life. I have no marriage, no friends, and no relationship with Noah and I've lost my ability to even just be a housewife. Why the hell won't this child just see I'm trying to love him? I'm trying so hard, activities, long deep conversations, one on one time with me. Please for god's sake just show me the way to a perfect parent haven! I do not like the child I gave birth too. I love him but he makes me feel useless.

Moses was put on Equasym xl and today was one of the extra bad days. Happy birthday Emma. This is one of those days where I wish I wasn't agnostic. Maybe God would take pity on me and turn me into Emma Plows the super mum!

Tuesday.

You see, school teachers have this strange ability of making you feel like your five again. Every time I pick my children up from school I look at the ground and try not to make eye contact. Most days it's 50/50 but it's generally the same "ohh it's been a bad one today Mrs Plows". I have always trusted in the support and the application of the interventions my sons have receives at school. Although I always appreciate daily updates and think they are vital, just what in the hell do you want me to do when my son has been a little shit? This sentence isn't a cop out, but really, you won't find a more involved, nosey, goby, interfering knowledgeable mother on this subject. So go ahead, tell me that Noah has kicked his teacher and you're telling me in the freezing cold in front of all the nosey mothers, what do you want me to do? Summons the autism fairy out of my backside?!

Wednesday. Do you ever wake up and think, I am going to really try today, really try to be the best mum? The mum I wish mine was. Maybe that kind of person doesn't exist.

Thursday. Inadvertently I feel like I emotionally neglect my son Moses. Sure I do all the things I'm supposed to do like feed him; say I love you and make him giggle. I love him but I don't like him a lot of the time. Maybe this is because I didn't bond with him for the first year of his life. There was just no attachment.

I want Noah. I want him to say I love you mummy, is that asking too much. Moses says it all the time which is lovely, but only when he wants something. I always do a little test in my head, if both my children were drowning, which would I save? I could never make a choice. I think that's a good thing because the day I could choose would be a very sad day. Am I a bad mum? Or just an honest one? Or just one that should stop thinking so much and ignore the pressure to be perfect?

Friday. This time of year (Christmas) really worries me. I always go high. For the first few days I can recognize my mood is changing, but if I leave it too long I get so ill I just stop being in control of my actions and take stupid risks. If however I get to the doctors quickly enough I can usually get sleeping tablets to stop the high. Success rate is about eighty per cent in my favour.

Saturday.

I'm going to sit on my fat arse and do nothing today. But if I play with the kids on the wii, one board game and twenty minutes of homework I will feel as though I have done my "good mum" bit for the day. Then I'm off on eBay to get a few Christmas presents. So even though I won't get out of my pyjamas I will have cleaned, shopped and been good mummy. Yeahhhh.

Sunday.

What will today bring? Ben is having a Krav Maga exam all day so I'm alone with the kids. As I lay here in bed I can hear the screams and there just from Ben. Shall I eat today? Maybe that will help me cope? Or bake Christmas biscuits for the family on xmas day. Maybe this is a temporary fake high. It's always a sign I'm going high when I start baking. Cupcakes, quiche, cheesecake and a torte is generally an afternoons worth. Well, let's see what hell or happiness the day of rest (Sunday) brings. Pork shoulder is a certainty!

Will Moses synapse take a firing break for a second to see the love I have to smother him with? Should it be love and hate with kids? There's absolutely NO hate with Noah. Is that because he's so vulnerable? Is that my fault? Are my feelings my fault? Do I love one more than the other? Or drenching Moses with that much love I'm neglecting Noah? I can't do that. And I can't win. Listening to what I'm reading out loud, I feel like an ungrateful cow but on the whole I do know how lucky I am. Beautiful children, a husband who has saved my life over and over again. But most of all, the good and bad times that have happened to me in my life have made me a better person. A good person. I can only be thankful for that.

The countdown to Christmas...

Monday. I dream, "why won't my son love me? Why won't he let me in and let me say the words?" I asked him how he would feel if I wasn't here anymore. He just replied "well I'd have more food, room and no one would nag me!" I know this sounds extreme, but it's just desperation. The shock factor doesn't work, and I don't want to use it. It's hard this time of year, change of routine makes me feel sick and anxious. Nothing is in its right place.

Tuesday.
I watched a programme today called "my child is not perfect", it was all about American kids with Autism. It's people who make it hard for parents, not the condition. People's ignorance is the tragedy, autism isn't the tragedy. Parents silly eye rolling assuming they can't "control" there child is the tragedy. Generally people don't understand or want to understand when it doesn't affect them. They just assume I can cope because it's all I have ever known. Don't say it's easy or hard for me; I'll be the judge of that!

Wednesday.
Moses has changed his entire Christmas list, again! I know it's inevitable that Christmas will have some tears. He's not supposed to take his medication on the weekend, and I hate giving him it as it is, but for the sake of the family and more importantly the sake of him, he needs to take it. I want to please him, make him like me; I know how desperate that sounds.

But at the end of the day, I am the parent and he is the child. Whether Moses is autistic or not, he still needs boundaries and discipline for my sake and especially for his.

Thursday.
Noah's birthday. For only the third time in Noah's life he cuddled me this morning. I cried. I gave him a huge hug and we watched transformers. Noah thought it would be amusing to make it sound like the transformers were passing wind robotically. I can't get into this child's head, but I can take what he's offering me and be grateful for that. On many an occasion I just watched and listened to him playing, my smile just got bigger and bigger with this blessing. He is so beautifully unique, I feel like such a lucky lady today. Noah loved all his presents and Moses was eager to play with him, and his new presents. At five o'clock we all went to pizza hut and ten of Noah's friends came for a party. He enjoyed himself and fell asleep holding his latest transformer.

Tonight I went into Moses's room and watched him sleep; I took a picture of him looking so peaceful and sweet. I smelt his skin and give him a tiny kiss on the cheek. Today was a good day.

Friday.

This evening I told Moses to get into bed forty six times. I didn't shout or scream. I put him into bed over and over again, but he's nine years old, should it really be like this? He told me he hated me twice. Forty six times aren't just numbers. Think about it could you do that in the space of two hours? I want to scream and cry but I can't complain, can I? Because apparently I'm bloody super mum! Or so some random mother I don't know told me today at school today. I know people are only trying to be nice, but seriously, save your pity for Oxfam. Trust me I know how good I am and how good I'm not. I won't ignore my children's pain, worries and concerns because I can't or won't deal with them. But I won't be (metaphorically) wiping their noses forever either! At night I just want them in my bed. To hold, cuddle and smell. Just to know there safe and happy. But it's hard because Moses shouts and screams and is hard to get close too and Noah won't really entertain me past 7pm. It's not routine.

Saturday.

Christmas Eve. Ben's dad came to stay for Christmas today came today, this cheered us all up as he lives near the coast and we all miss him a lot. He always comes to us this time of year and visits Ben's sister and niece when he's here too. Even though the last days have been quite anxious I've started to calm down. I must admit the doctor did give me some medication! I was determined to sit down with the kids and play a board game today. When you see two autistic boys laugh for just a few minutes, it kind of just fills up my happy count. And I can deal with the rest of the day. But know, there were lots of last minute things I'd forgotten, I must make my new year's resolution to be more organised. Or more perfect. Still, I had to smile, Moses had built a Lego game in his room with dungeons and trap doors, and he had great pride in his face. Whenever I see this face it reminds me that I'm actually doing an ok job.

Sunday.
Christmas day. Every year all the family goes up to my mums house where all five generations meet up. My brother calls it the "smash and grab" as everyone gets a gift for everyone. Today was no exception. Gifts fly everywhere and its lovely but people can't afford it. I think they should just stick to making it all about the kids. This year, for my mum, I sent some money to Oxfam to provide fifty condoms

for people in Africa. She in turn bought me a goat of an African village.

Noah had pizza for dinner (he only usually eats round things) Moses wouldn't eat because of his meds. I'd been picking all day, in-law eats like a mouse because he's old and Ben had a fair bit. So lots of turkey curries. The kids just wanted to be alone all day and play in their own worlds, which they seemed to enjoy. We did get one board game, a Lego one, and I got my autism laughs. Today was a good day.

Monday.

Today we went to an all you can eat Chinese. These are good for my kids because of the variety. Moses and Noah notices a woman with no legs or arms and they looked for a second and Moses said to Noah "just because someone's disabled doesn't mean that they can't do everything everyone else can do you know" " I know that Moses, I'm not stupid, they can go up Everest and run in the Olympics with them bendy legs and everything" I was proud today. Just when you think you're not getting through you have these break through moments of parental pride.

Tuesday. I sit down on the sofa and he shuffles away from me. If I discipline him he holds it against me for days and I don't know when it will end. All I want is normality. Is that too much to ask? I feel selfish saying that, I really do. Who am I to demand that my life should run like everyone else's? I went to see my psychiatrist today. I go to a private hospital that I can't afford but, in all honesty there's no one lower in the NHS food chain than people with mental health problems. Anyway I told him about my Christmas worries and he wanted to put me on an anti-psychotic. Been there done that! Those things in my opinion should only be taken if absolutely necessary as they physically disable you. I'll stick to the Valium as and when I need it. And with my strict aversion to drugs this is a very rare occasion.

Wednesday. Tonight we are going to see one of Ben's friends. They believe one of their child has Autism. I'm always happy to meet new people relating to autism, not socially because I find that makes me really anxious. Anyway I get worried because Moses will almost defiantly be rude. This makes me feel sick as I'm always apologising for him. God I hope they are nice people; I'd love to get to know another mother who can relate to what I can. I just hope my own social skills kick in and I snap into interesting talkative Emma.

Thursday.
Wow they were just like us. She was in her forty's but looked my age, she's had five children and realised something wasn't right with one of them. The problem I have is, a woman with five children really would have a good insight into Nero typical behaviour. But still doctors told her she was wrong. Basically I'm saying "mother knows best" and doctors don't give parents nowhere near enough credit. She's got it hard with her son's school, there giving him detention three times a week for not doing singing, dancing and doing sport. All of which, generally, autistic people don't do, won't do and can't do. So he's getting detention for having autism! Do we really live a world where people with disabilities are treated and so misunderstood like this? This is wrong. Moses was really good. I was proud of him and I told him that.

Friday.
Didn't sleep well as Ben was snoring and I was talking in my sleep. How the hell do I wake myself up talking crap? Not a great combination. Anyway I took a sleeping tablet at 2pm. Not good. I'm knackered so I, Noah and

Moses watched a Christmas film while they fiddled with their Lego. It was peaceful and Moses cuddled up to me like a purring kitten. I got a tear in my eye. Closeness to a child is the most precious gift you will get from them. Their smell, their warmth, their heartbeat……………………………………….and then the wet patch of slobber on your new top when you realise they've fallen asleep.

Saturday.
Today we took the kids up to a local manor house with a farm attached to walk the dog. I love it there, the old manor house, the numerous acres of land and the farm and park. We had a really nice walk around and stretched our legs, I always feel like a "real" family when we do this. Whatever the hell that means. Afterwards we went to this really cute tea room in the courtyard. We sat down with our tea and biscuits and juice for the kids. Suddenly a baby started crying, but really shrieking like it had colic. Noah especially hates loud noises and I knew this was going to be a problem. Moses quickly remarked "can't you shut that baby up" I told him to be quiet but Noah was crying and had his hands on his ears and was rocking back and forth. The people heard Moses and as we hastily left the mother said "god haven't they ever heard a baby cry,

take your freaky kids then" I lost it. I went up to the table (Ben took the kids) and got right down to her level. I told her that my sons were both autistic and couldn't cope with the noise, this wasn't her fault but it was best we left. She looked very apologetic and it went quiet. I smiled, stood up and said "if you ever call my kids freaky again I will rip your head off and stuff it up your husband's arse!" I smiled and left. Quickly! I am not proud of my behaviour and I can't justify it. Every parent should defend their child but when a child has a disorder and can't defend themselves it's extremely hard to keep it together. Or maybe that's just me.

Sunday.
I'm baking. Its happening isn't it I know it is. I am going high. Two quiches, twenty four cupcakes, steak and ale pie with black pudding, twelve chocolate brownies and a pavlova. I'm knackered but I am still smiling like a bloody idiot. Right, it's eleven in the morning, Sunday lunch to start. Do you ever decide that today I am going to make a memory? I used to have a lovely friend in my life that isn't around anymore. And whenever we did daft stuff, which was often because I hadn't yet been diagnosed and she was just barmy. Anyway sometimes I decide I'm going to make a memory and

somehow capture a moment in time in my head that I can go back too whenever I was sad. So, one of the best ones was when my mate had decided that she was going to clean a garden of an empty council house so that she could very "slyly" dig up and steal the six very established, eight foot , conifers. I remember just stood facing the house with a Tesco bag in my hand cleaning up the crap from someone else's garden and seeing Veronica digging up a tree with a trowel. A TROWL! She bloody did it too. Well one of them. We had a good laugh and stuck it in the back of her car; she dumped it in the back garden and left it to die. That makes me laugh. You see when your bipolar everything seems like such a great idea at the time but then bang! No interest the next. This memory makes me smile. I miss her; she was one of my allies.

Monday.

Noah went to the bathroom today. Fifteen minutes later I called him and asked what he was doing. He told me there was no toilet paper and he was just waiting for some. He hadn't told me he needed some. He came upon an obstacle but didn't tackle it. He just sat there. I don't really know what to think about that. I still think I'm going high. My brain is going faster than my mouth which means I'm talking crap and think

I'm really interesting. I don't really want to go out and I'm scared to meet any neighbours because although I have lots of friends I know where I am with them. I don't need or want anymore "friends". Generally I'm very happy and practically go skipping down the street smiling at people I never speak too. I really don't want to risk striking up a conversation of SHITE! So I'm staying a recluse at the moment.

Tuesday.

I sometimes wonder if my mum has bipolar, it's not as though her symptoms are sitting up and waving at me but because I don't know my dad I just look for the symptoms and signs. I remember as a child she could be nice one minute and then really cold the next. That affects you as a kid, you become insecure and nervous. I'm glad I eventually got help. The ones that don't are misunderstood and don't get the best out of life.

Wednesday.

I haven't been properly high for about five years now. I think it's because myself and Ben are getting so good at recognising it, so therefore usually been able to stop or lesson the blow with Valium and sleeping tablets. Being high isn't good, but it isn't the worst thing in the world either. You're really happy and you want to save the world. Well I am anyway; I can't speak for everyone with the condition. I also get very vain, over confidant, have copious amounts of energy and anger and believe I can achieve anything. I smile at one thing I did which wasn't funny really. I was waiting for a parking space but a man stole it. I got out and I told him if he didn't move that I would block him in and I was doing my full weekly shop and would be some time. He laughed and walked off. I remember pouring paint stripper all over his car and then driving to Asda instead. Did I do that to the Mr Aston Martin man? Or did I just imagine it? Both are possible. I suppose I'll never know!

Thursday. Five times we had to get up last night with Moses. He takes medication at night which is generally effective. We went from getting up six times to only two. I hope this isn't a new trend. Anyway hospital appointment next month, hopefully someone will finally find a solution to our "night terror issue".

Friday. Well we've been invited to the only neighbour I interact with tonight with Ben and the kids. My son is their son's friend so at least they'll play together. I hope. I'm really not in the mood for smiles and conversations about kids but she seems nice enough so a very rare glass of wine may loosen me up.

Saturday.
Homebrew my arse! I'm not a drinker as it is but three sips of that cleaning fluid is enough to make my pee that potent it could clean the oven. But in all honesty I know nothing of wine and I may just have very poor taste buds. The kids played well with her little ones and that always makes me smile. I'm glad I went because they seem really genuine and down to earth. I've been invited back tonight for new year's eve but it's all so much effort and I have been feeling so down lately so whenever I'm sad I always surround myself with the things I like that make me feel special. I love my bed because its king size and has a huge quilt. Six big pillows and 14 bed pillows. I put on my flower bomb perfume, get into my soft PJ's, have my laptop and eat cheese. Some people drink beer, I eat cheese in bed.

Sunday. HAPPY NEW YEAR.
Is it silly to think 2012 will be good because I like the ring on the year. 2012 2012 2012. Off to mum and dads today, they live with Luke my brother. My kids really love my mum and dad but I kind of think it's because they feed them

shit freezer food. You know the crap you get at budget weddings, but really does fill that hole in your belly when you're bored and pissed. Anyway off to my sons idols that can't do any wrong but in my eyes could never do any right.

It could be said that in today's society we actually look for disorders. We have a fascination with "making things right". As though we all have to be the same and we are scared or just plain wrong if we are not the same. It's the same with death. If a person dies at 65. that's young is it? We can't all live to one hundred. We have to die or resources run out. We need natural disasters. I know this sounds bloody harsh but the things that are happening in the world because of overpopulation are very unnerving. Anyway rant over. Is it evolution? Were we all once autistic or ADHD? Are we over cautious? In my experience "professionals" or doctors are under cautious, or maybe they just don't like giving bad news.

Monday. I woke up in absolute despair today. When I opened my eyes I was crying. I don't know why, it wasn't a dream, I just feel so sad. So Valium for breakfast and I was coping with the day in no time. Still a bit teary though. It's annoying when you're down for no reason. If

someone was dying or there was a real tragedy I'd have a reason to feel like this, but I'm not doing this to me it's just happening to me. I can't stop it, it's just there and I want the horrible darkness to lift because I'm not prepared to take Valium every day. [Smash here in case of Valium emergency]

Tuesday....................sick

Wednesday...............still sick

Thursday.
My two blessings encroached on me and changed my life. I obliviously lived as an ignorant woman. I became slightly wiser, stronger and happier as my life started to have a purpose. Life educated me. Education can come in many forms. Whether it is a degree or being an apprentice or just plain life's tragedies or good fortune. It can all be positive or negative when life is the one that throws it at you. I got lucky. I used to be a very ignorant woman. A woman who believed that autism and ADHD where "naughty labels". I would often call people nutters because they didn't speak or look the same as me. Who the hell was I? I was supposed to receive these children. They were meant to be mine. I'm not too

sure if it was god. But would god really send a woman two autistic boys who couldn't smile? Couldn't laugh? Couldn't enjoy? Couldn't fight? And believe me, you have to fight. Nothing comes easy to the parents of autistic children. Ben didn't believe Noah was autistic. He thought I was mad because I was suffering from postnatal depression. Many friends and family told me that Noah was fine and it was all in my head. But they lied to me; secretly they agreed with me but were trying to put me at ease. All they did was make me feel like I was going mad, I was right, I was right because I knew best. Not one person apologised to me when he was finally diagnosed. If anyone ever reads this, you know who you are!

Friday.

I'm not making myself cry. I don't want to scream, scratch myself or burn my hand on the kettle. Feeling like this is crap but Bipolar is happening to me and it's not a choice I can control. I can honestly say at times in my life I have not been responsible for my own actions. This was many years ago but still I have glitches. Not that I'm a ticking time bomb, I just have spare of the moment mishaps shall I say. Today was a sad day. I found £20 in the washer. It was still a sad day.

Saturday.
Am I getting well? How do I know if I'm ok? I haven't cried today, but the lithium won't let me. I've been taking Valium regularly but I've taken less today. I tried to set a target, a kind of "let's make today worthwhile" day. I set a target of walking to the shop for some milk. Instead I did the ironing and planted some daffodil bulbs. Not the same but I did something that needs doing and I felt like my day was not a wasted day. I don't like wasting days. There precious.

Sunday.
Noah and Moses woke me up with a cup of tea and egg on toast. That made me smile. The next two hours of Walle in my bed with the family didn't, but it was nice to hear them laugh and feel the warmth of their skin in there Jim jams. I think I'm on the mend. I was only up twice with Moses. Yahhh!

If only I could wake today so wonderful,

Like a perfect 1940s housewife but not so dull.

Be able to cope with kids, friends and concentration,

A wonderful life living out my imagination.

My children have smiles I have no piles

And people do as I say without objection.

Useless bitch.

Monday. Moses wants to love Noah, but Noah won't let him because the cuddles make him sad. It's very hard for an autistic child to understand the world, so how can I expect one autistic child to understand another autistic child? Nature or life, will take its course and we will see how they are in a decade. One thing I do know is that there is great love there; I just don't think they know it yet.

Tuesday. I generally don't get to see the effects of Moses medication. Equasym helps Moses a lot but only for around five hours a day so as he only has it at Monday to Friday we get the hyperactive difficult Moses. I hate calling him difficult. I mean unique, imaginative, clever, and odd; I don't know, just hard, hard work. Every day, when I make his bed, I put a couple of books on his tidy bed. Last thing at night I go in and read his books with him. Space, snakes and fleabag monkey face. I like those moments. I hold on to those moments.

Wednesday.

PlayStation, Xbox, Wii, Nintendo DS, television in their bedrooms, DVD players, computers, mobile phones and letting them off eating their sweet corn. No wonder child discipline is going to the dogs!

Thursday.

I woke this morning feeling like I have absolutely no friends. Well apart from Ben. It seems like everyone has their own lives and I am just plodding along. I'd say I have acquaintances, you no, you could go round for a coffee but it would have to be booked two weeks in advance because people are so so busy and I am, well, not. In all honesty, friends wear me out and I find them a huge effort. Still would be nice to have a few more, just to know they were there. Maybe it's me; maybe I'm not trying hard enough.

Friday.

I didn't leave the house today. I'm kind of psyching myself up for the first day back at school on Tuesday, dentist and plead for chill out meds from the doctor. Uurghh! Not looking forward to it but hey it could be worse; I could be booked in to have my haemorrhoids burnt off with a soldering iron. I have four kids in the house at the moment, Noah upstairs playing transformers and Moses and his mates playing war hammer in the conservatory. Moses loves letting other kids know all about war and combat. You'd think he had won the Victoria Cross in the war!

Saturday.
So, done a bit of shopping today and got a great cheap coat for Noah. He's off on an adventure trip with the school next Wednesday for three days and I've been sorting out the packing for him and Ben as he's also going as an assistant. I'll miss them a hell of a lot but I'm really looking forward to spending some time with Moses by myself. My mum and I have promised to take him to a "posh" restaurant. He pulls a face but I know he likes things like that.

Sunday.
I'm over stimulated. Is that the problem? Was it that all along and I'm not bipolar. You see. People with simple lives who don't continually analyse everything seem a lot happier. Jesus. Fuck it I could be dead tomorrow. I've never been a talker I have always been a doer. I find it very frustrating when I hear people complain about things that could easily be rectified with just a little effort. Am I one of those people? Are all of us?

Monday. The frustration in me is intense. It feels warm and makes me nauseous. I hear parents say "no means no" I get it but Moses will never learn that. I'm a fairly strict parent more so because I want my children to feel secure and know how to handle a situation. If I say no and I never back down then they know no means no right? Noah yes Moses no. Moses isn't able to be conditioned. It's hard with Moses but you know I think he's going to be ok because he's sharp, funny and assertive. So what if he's cheeky to Mrs Tate, That kid has got character!

Tuesday. I knew when I woke this morning that Noah was worrying and a bit tearful. As we took him to school as soon as he got into his class he let out his speech in tears. "Mrs. Tate, I just want you to know that I hate you and if you take just one more golden time point off of me I will blow up the school and destroy you". With a clenched fist he yelled," VICTORY IS MINE!" At the time the teacher just looked discussed and shook her head. Oh but you know she's been on a course so she's so up on the autism thing! Yeah, and I'm a size zero! When we picked him up he was crying and very annoyed. I really think it's time we got some advice on been able to control his temper.

Wednesday.

My big boy. Huge eyes chubby cheeks and an infectious giggle. I've always believed that Noah was a gift, as though I'd known him in a past life and he's here to guide me and make my life have a special purpose. I'm not really a believer in all that bible bashing palaver but I like the romance of the idea. Moses I know is here to keep me strong. He challenges me but I think that keeps me determined. He's my cuddle machine. And I love his cuddles.

Thursday.

I've never blamed my parents for the way I am but sometimes, and I mean rarely, I am very aware that my behaviour is very probably because there was so much expressed emotion in the home. My dad boomed his frightful voice up the stairs for the silliest of things, like if I'd left crumbs on the kitchen side. He hovered over me when I washed up, wiped the kitchen tops when making toast (our staple diet) and spewed out continuous sarcastic criticisms. I was a wreck and developed terrible OCD. Maybe this is why I can't take criticism and hate shouting and will avoid it at all costs. My mum never cuddled me, took us anywhere or showed any emotion. I know I know Boo fucking hoo. I love both my mum and dad and I don't want to sound like a Jeremy Kyle victim by blaming my behaviour on my parents but my upbringing was everything I don't want for my sons. There were many emotionally sad times and especially one horrific part of my childhood that I won't go into out of respect of my parents. Plus there are some family who are unaware of it.

We are all a product of our upbringing but we can change this. We can blame the rest of the world for our problems of accrue the wisdom and become wiser people. I've inherited the bad and the good influences for my upbringing. Some people just don't know how to parent. I try my best. And mum and dad did too. Xxx

Friday.
We analyse so much in the days we exist in this life. Why am I here? Who am I? Am I a good mum? Should I use vegetable oil or olive oil to fry my bacon in? We analyse that much we forget to bloody live this precious healthy life most of us have been given. Everyone always says when someone dies.... "Live everyday like it's your last because you don't know when it's going to end." Well I won't wait until someone passes. I

realises that as much as I can right now. Olive oil!! I'll go with that.

Saturday.

Ben's took the kids to see his dad today and I've been feeling a bit reflective. I like my own company and I always feel I get a very satisfying conversation talking to just myself. That sentence made me smile. I've often looked at my life and thought what have I achieved? When I had Moses, Noah was nearly two. I was told I had post-natal depression, then depression, then attachment disorder. Then dissociate personality disorder. Then after seeing my BUPA saviour Dr Wong, finally I was told I had Bipolar. This took two years and a lot of money. Money I didn't have but money well spent.

Within two years I truly believed Noah had Autism. Nobody listened apart from my mum. Everyone said I was ill and I was being silly. Even Ben thought I was mad and contradicted me in front of doctors all the time. I had a fight on my hands and I started to stop talking about it. I contacted the National Autistic Society and after six months they sent a specialist speech and language therapist to my home when Ben was at work. I paid her £100 cash and she watched Noah for an hour. But the best thing she did was listened more than she talked and I always think that's an excellent attribute for a health professional. She agreed with me and she sat and cried with me. She wrote a letter to my son's psychologist and six months later after only forty five minutes he was diagnosed with Asperger's syndrome. NO ONE ever apologised for making out I was mad. Uneducated morons! Am I bitter? It wasn't the label I needed it was the help that came with the label. That fight brought me out of depression and I finally started to bond with Moses. This is so far my biggest life achievement. This isn't a hard statement, but trust your instincts and never give up. No one knows better than a mother.

Sunday. In the past Valium has saved my life. It's saved me from hurting other people too. Before I got help, I was a very ill woman who could and did snap at any minute. Many months from my past are lost from my memory and maybe for the best. But every now and then one pops up and I have to re-evaluate who I am yet again. People and doctors will throw it at you or ban it but for me it's been a plaster when I've needed it. I can't complain about wanting it now and then when I can't cope because unfortunately although I have and can go years without it it's still my safety net. People do coke, vodka or self-harm. I survive. And I survive well. As I look back I'm happy with what I've achieved. It's startling at how far I've come, how I developed through the hardest of times.

Does bipolar mean I am a mental case?

Just because my brain doesn't run at the normal pace.

My memory is terrible, why do I bother?

My thoughts skip from one to another.

My mouth is slow and my thoughts are faster,

All my pills are only my plaster,

I'll try to get better, I have no choice,

But this will only happen if you hear my voice.

Am I getting there?

Monday. Today I've been in that mood where I just want sex. I've read that people with Bipolar become sex addicts. I didn't. But sometimes you just need to fill the hole, metaphorically speaking of course. Now I don't know why I'm writing that, I'm in the mood but I think sometimes I like to be seen as a sexual woman rather than Mrs Plows, Mum, Or are lass! I'm just thinking out loud. It's been a funny day today. I've bought some nice underwear from Debenhams and we'll see where my sex obsession ends up today. Brace yourself Ben.

Tuesday. I had a wonderful phone call from a woman I've been in contact with relating to her son who may have autism. She called to say he had been diagnosed. I wept slightly when she told me, I was so pleased for her. It may seem a strange thing been happy at an Autism diagnosis but it's the certainty of a mothers knowledge and been continually ignored and the fight to get to the end, or beginning whichever way you want to look at it that brings it all together. I WAS RIGHT. Now help my boy!

Wednesday.

Today's been a funny day. It's been well, good. I've felt in control of the things I have had to do and planed my day well. I went to Asda and did a shop for two weeks and didn't spend over one hundred and twenty pounds. I was thrifty and sensible. The reason I am so detailed today about my mundane shopping is because I'm realising I have been spending more than usual. Spending isn't good. I've bought six dresses, loads of clothes for the kids, a chandelier and only pants for Ben, all on eBay. I'm paranoid this is a high blip but I'm going to try and concentrate on something different. Gardening I think!

Thursday.

A lady I have been helping regarding her autistic son was told by the senco (special education needs coordinator) that the school had done as much as they could and where willing to do for her son and it was advised to keep the thirteen year old at home. Do we really live in a society where the education system gives up because it's too much hassle to educate a child who doesn't see the world in the same way the rest of us do? Every child has the right to an education and an autistic child has the right to have an education that is designed through the curriculum for them. Each child is a blessing; these aren't just words because every child can give something to the world and receive so much back. Each child affects someone else's life and leaves lasting positive memories with them. Where's the passion? Why don't people go the extra mile anymore? Urgh! Is all I have to say to that silly senco's ridiculous negative statement.

Friday.
So I woke up at seven and took 20 milligrams (yes that's what I was told to take) of diazepam in preparation of my filling putting in at the dentist at 815am. Jesus! Where did today go? I don't know, but I have a lovely white filling. I think I went down the dentist steps on my bum browsing Facebook on my blackberry. Ahhhh what a day!

Saturday.
You know when you get those little letters in your child's book bags saying "a child in the class has had head lice"? Well I always throw them away because my sons have really short hair and I never believed they would

catch lice. Anyway, out comes his teacher yesterday as she always does and pulls me to one side, as she always does and says "Noah has lice". Ok, I said I'd have a look and check us all. I wasn't embarrassed because I didn't believe it and well nits is a fact of life. I got home and put a nit comb through Noah's hair, as he screamed because I'd touched his head (Noah has sensory problems which means he over or under feels sensations and pain) masses of live nits fell out on to his neck. Ah, I stayed quiet and over the next two hours we all had the nit treatment. Well I am glad that's all over; my children seriously think I was physically abusing them. Thank god we no longer use Derbac and Thank god they don't know Ester Ransons number!

Sunday.

It's amazing that the word "Sunday" (Just like Mondays) can change people's mood. Walks in the park with the dog and time with family. Today I didn't want to go out into the world and see people. I had to go see my mum because it's my brother Aiden's birthday tomorrow and I had gifts to drop off. Every now and then my mum really gets on my nerves and I get rather upset. Of course all this goes back to my childhood; I hate it when people blame their childhood for the downfalls of the rest of their lives. I always feel like she's going to let me down. I always feel like I am there for her more than she is for me. I don't think that's just a feeling, it's definite. Who knows what goes on in my mums head but the only qualities I got from my mum is well "mental issues". But what's the point in dwelling on roundabout feelings that won't, and can't change? I don't know but just like everyone else ill still always have my hang-ups. Maybe that makes me who I am, the good and the bad. I went up to mums and yes she wanted a lift to Iceland, I didn't mind I got some bits and saw my dad and Luke.

I have bipolar, it doesn't have me,

I also have dyslexia, constipation and sometimes leak wee.

Sometimes I'm high sometimes I'm low,

When I'm high I bake and laugh, because that's what I know.

Its only when I'm low that I stress,

Who knows what will happen and what ill confess.

Bear with me I'm actually very nice,

Been my friend and giggling with me is no sacrifice.

Quality time with Moses.

Monday. God I have nice boobs.

Tuesday. Well the day before Noah's trip and I generally get a bit scared knowing I am going to be on my own at night. I'm ok at the moment and I know I'm going to miss them but I have planned a few things for Moses and I to do and my mum keeps making plans too because she very obviously takes favouritism over Moses more than Noah. I think it's because Moses is unruly and cheeky and she thinks that's cute. Noah is more obviously autistic and doesn't understand the world let alone my mum so certainly doesn't understand his grandma. Ben's mum also does this but I have no interest in that. It's my mum that upsets me when she does this. It's just not right. She then has the nerve to say I do more for Noah because I buy him anything. That's my mums way of showing love, spending!. Noah grows very fast as he's so tall and puts weight on so quickly so I am constantly on eBay buying clothes for him. Moses gets just as many clothes but he also get all Noah's too. He must have five times the clothes Noah has. You know when people say "do you have a favourite?" I really don't. I sometimes think people confuse favouritism with preferring certain quality's in their children. Also maybe parents understand certain vulnerabilities in them that make a parent exude different emotions towards the child, but maybe this isn't having a "favourite".

Wednesday.
Do you remember when I mentioned making memories? I've just remembered a funny one. My brother Josephs wife Millie and I used to get on quite well (not that we don't now) and I really wasn't well. I think at

this point I was having my first high. The problem with big highs and not what I call mini highs is that you get an awful lot of memory loss. I do however remember been very excited for some reason and with Millie been such a lively character I didn't think for a minute anything was wrong. Ben was in with the kids who were two and six months and I decided I wanted to go for a walk. It was raining, a lot and Millie and I decided to go look for puddles to jump in. I went a whole step further and started trying to swim in the puddles. I remember laughing with Millie at how daft this was but we just kept walking the dark wet streets for puddles. What really makes me laugh it that Millie was in her work suit. I was ill, what was her excuse? Shed laugh at that. We had fun that night, we made a memory. I'm smiling right now, but I think you had to be there.

Thursday.
Some days I wake up and I know I am already in a rage. A quite solid wall structure consumes in my earthly being. Throughout the day it starts to materialise into the open where others also become aware of it. If you speak to me or look at me, you've said or looked at me wrongly and you're trying to annoy me and make me angry. You're stupid and idiotic and nowhere near as superior as me. So do as I

say and they won't be a fucking problem will there!? Today's a bad day.

Friday.
I've just read yesterdays "effort". I'm fine today and I am really excited to go to Centre Parcs in a couple of weeks. It does worry me that one day I can be fine and the next really not right. I think I'm going to speak to my doctor about my mood.

Saturday.
I left Ben in bed this morning and took the kids to the park. They woke up at seven so I thought it best I didn't wake the whole house. At seven thirty the park was dead. A fresh morning with our fleece jumpers on, there's something about keeping your kids warm and dry and watching them have fun. I feel like I'm really doing my job right. I sometimes think that's why I was put on this earth, to learn to be a good mum. I'm always learning.

Sunday.
Chicken defrosting, floor clean of dog hairs, ironing done, well some of it and snuggles with Ben on the sofa. Blissful day, I wish Noah would stop asking me for a cup of Joe. Honestly he is so easily influenced by television, and his dad.

Monday.

I've had a pretty vain day today. I've dyed my hair, had it cut, had my nails done and done a whole load of, well just looking in the mirror. I don't even know if I'm actually as good looking as I think I am. Looks fade, especially with women. Women should always use their brain first and foremost to get to where they want to be in life because one day there looks won't have the same effect on the world as they once did. I know that sounds harsh and sounds as though I'm saying women have nothing if there not pretty, but that's not what I'm saying. The fact is women shouldn't rely on their looks to make their mark on the world because the world is a fickle place.

Tuesday.

These were just a few of Noah's symptoms that I noticed at the age of two, I thought I'd share them.

1. No babbling or pointing.
2. no single words or two-word phrases
3. No response to name
4. Very minimum language and social skills
5. Poor eye contact
6. Obsessive lining up of toys, objects and food.
7. No smiling or social responsiveness.

8. No imaginative play.

Wednesday.
Ben and Noah went on a school trip today. I'm missing them already but I am really looking forward to quality time with Moses. So, its pizza hut with mum and Moses tonight. Noah was so excited, especially because he had been put in a group with his three best mates, I love seeing the smile on his face, full of hope and excitement. This morning I sat him down and I put his head in my hands and said "now Noah, over the next few days remember every fun time you have and hold onto it in your head. That's making a memory, and you're going to make lots and lots" that made us both smile.

Thursday.
Today was a great day; I walked up to school with Moses with the dog and then took the dog for a little walk in the woods near bye. Every now and then I feel really strong and capable, that's how I felt today because I had no one to rely on. Although I can look after myself, because I am a big girl, I have been in a relationship since I was fourteen years old and without shoving woman's liberation straight into a miss world contest, I honestly sometimes thing I'm not strong enough to be single. I know that's

sad. It's a good job I am happily married then I suppose. Not that that's always been the case.

Friday.
Noah and Ben came home today and I couldn't wait to see them. Moses and I had a great time but it feels so alien to me when my family isn't all together at home. Noah had a great time but I think Ben had a better one. Ben is going to be a great primary school teacher. I know he's finding collage difficult, but that's the idiotic gobshites! Or so he calls them. He loves the work and I hope he gets into university. He will, I have a lot of faith in that man.

Lord show me how to be a good mum, much better than my own,

Let the world know that my child's not dumb, and that I not dare to moan.

I can be so much better I know, I just crave a little assistance to help me glow,

So I can go the distance.

Saturday.

I really do understand how fine the line is between smacking and not smacking. I don't take that route. I believe if smacking worked you'd only ever have to do it once and I think very few parents could admit to that. I believe if I ever smacked one of my children it would be out of my own anger and id go way too far. It's hard to be restraint when a child really pushes you too far.

Sunday.

Moses's behaviour is getting worse; this isn't a figure of my imagination. I can speak the whole autism thing. The rules, the compassion and patience. With Noah I can certainly walk the walk, with Moses? I don't know how this frustration, crying and head banging will work out. And that's just me!

Monday.

Yeahhhhhhh. Holidays. It's a shame it forecast rain all week but in all honest cabin it up in the woods is hardly lounging on Bondi beach. I'm really excited. I just can't wait for that quality time with my three boys and no dog! You know I think it's a lot colder in the woods, and its bloody snowing!

Tuesday.

Well today has been one of those really great days that I think I'll remember for a very long time. I booked lots of activities and made sure we didn't do too much hanging around. So a fun packed day of tree trekking, hawk perching, archery, swimming and a facial for me was just the ticket for a great start to a relaxing family holiday.

Wednesday.

I missed my lithium last night and I woke up this morning after a crappy night's sleep feeling a bit down. You see been "a bit down" isn't the end of the world, people feel like this all the time but when you have bipolar everything is either very desensitised or emotions and moods are very magnified. I really needed to have a little cry but because the lithium is slow release that emotion doesn't come easy. We cry for a reason, I assume to release pent up emotions but when you can't, depression can kick in. We through the word depression around all the time and seems to be very over used. But real depression is so debilitating it can seriously effect, or end someone's life. I asked Ben to take the kids swimming and hypnotised myself (I can do that) back to sleep. When I woke I felt a little better. I forced myself to go play mini golf in the rain with the kids and played photographer. I'm smiling at the pictures now. Today ended much better than it started.

Thursday.

It's the last night of our cabin forest and I'm trying to hold on to my memories to take home with me. Its rain for all of the holiday but one good thing about the British is that even in the rain we still make the most of a holiday, we have to otherwise we wouldn't have any. I remember when I was about ten and we went on a family holiday to primrose valley. We stayed in a static caravan and it continually rained for a week. My mum was insistent we went to the beach. So we all walked down the cliff to the beach with our matching homemade shorts on that my mum had made from my grandmothers old curtains, with bags, sandwiches and raincoats. We set up camp, in the rain surrounded by three windbreakers in our coats, gloves and hats on but no socks and shoes eating Haslet sandwiches. Well we had to get the beach experience!

Friday.

Every day on this holiday we have had maid service. I hate maid service, people just barge in and start nicking your towels because you've used them once. Call me a scruff but I don't clean my towels every day. Anyway, in waltzed a, let's say "bubbly" looking women with egg mayonnaise down her tabard screaming

MORNING, I wasn't in the mood. I asked "can I help you?" in a rather sarcastic voice, she told me she was an early riser, she was allergic to her new cat, her mums over for a visit and told me that I could probably tell she was a Virgo. I replied "Yes it shows that you believe in the delusion that a person's life is somehow affected by the position of the sun and moon! Oops. It's one of those "say as you see it days". The lady then proceeded to ha ha ha ha ha in a voice not actually fitting her earlier one. Oh lord, take me home.

Saturday.

Does every woman have hairy toes? Well I have. Granted I shave them, I mean I might get run over and have my feet on a stretcher. Then all I have to worry about is my mucky pants.

Sunday.

I did something today that I hadn't done in many years. I went to the Salvation Army. I was raised in the Salvation Army and although I left at the age of fourteen it was a second family to me. It showed me how real healthy families behave. I'm agnostic, I believe in god but I feel very uncomfortable with organised religion. Anyway, I woke up this morning feeling rather sombre and reflective. I felt really grateful for what I have. I'm so very lucky to have the family I have. So I went to the Salvation Army I used to go to in the next town Beeston. As soon as I walked in the meeting hall I was met by so many faces that I recognised me and that I remember too. I felt like I was at home. I did a lot of smiling. It's funny how bringing yourself home to some safe comfortable places can make you feel really protected. Everything seems so clear. Today was a good day.

Tuesday.

If someone professes to be smart, and actually openly says "I am smart". Is that not the definition of not been smart? I mean that's just silly arrogance. Arrogance is not smart. I say this only because I met a girl today that told me that she could get any man because she exudes confidence and the more she tells men she's "really smart" the more they love it. I must point out this girl was a girl, well, twenty. Some people say things and there are just no words. I could have given her a big speech or even told her she was plain stupid but I think people need a few knock backs in their life. Having real life experience and filtering out the wisdom and positives can only make the best of us much better people.

Wednesday. We had a hospital appointment at the general hospital today with Moses, we have to have so many appointments that take the children out of school, but then we get earache from the school as soon as we want to take them out for the afternoon. Note to self, I must look up section four of the 2010 Equality Act.

Thursday. I think I try not to get close to people because I expect far too much from them. People let you down and that infuriates me and upsets me. Also I hate been criticised and it can put me into very deep depression so I tend to avoid people who get off been rude. I only end up kicking off if I can't keep my composure. Falling on deaf ears is not the phrase. It's more like "are you deliberately trying to upset me?"

Friday. I've been having a lot of back pain today so it's been rather uneventful. Oh well my life can't be champagne and dancing girls all the time.

Saturday. Today was my grandfather's birthday; I always look forward to this night, mainly because I love having a big family. Every year we go to the local Cantonese. Fourteen of us were packed around two tables. My uncles new girlfriend was there and she absolutely lovely but she kept swearing. It was really funny. My grandmother kept looking really shocked and rolling her eyes. There's something very amusing about observing people in an environment that makes them feel uncomfortable but have to combine this with been polite. Not that I relish in my relatives been uncomfortable. The night was full of laughs and I got to spend time with my brother, which is rare. We do this every year and I love any reason for the family to get together. There were seventeen of us and that is by no means the whole family. We all live very close to each other, most of them live on the same estate I was raised on in Middleton. We all had a good laugh and I could tell my granddad loved it. I love my grandma and granddad so much; I can always go to them for a cuddle if I want one. When my dad had a stroke a couple of years ago and lost the majority if his speech I made my granddad promise he'd never die. I often feel guilty about making me promise me that.

Sunday.

I've been thinking that I wouldn't mind some nice (slightly erotic) pictures of myself before my tits and arse go even more south. I don't think I have the guts though and it seems a bit frivolous.

Monday.
It's so hard sometimes to not get frustrated with Moses. He won't take his new medication so we've had to start opening the capsules and putting the granules in a small amount of water. He took it and I told him how proud I was at him. He rewarded me with a big toothy smile and said he loves me and I am the most beautiful mummy in the world. We then had a half an hour discussion regarding the fact that he loves me more than I love him and I couldn't possibly love him more. He's one argumentative head strong boy. I can't think where he gets that from.

Tuesday.
Why do we continually torture ourselves to achieve the perfect weight and size? I actually love having a big arse and big knockers. That's what women should look like right. Are we counting the points and calories for us, or someone else? Well I'm not going to diet unless I actually am overweight. So I'm going to stick to my size twelve jeans and sod everyone else..
well, size fourteen, I like them baggy!

Wednesday.

I have to be really honest about my thoughts. This is because my diary is my emotional outlet and I am very aware that I could evolve this piece of righting into a very controversial piece of ignorant drivel. When other parents and the public encounter a person with autism, the knowledge of the condition is very limited and inaccurate. Because of this, and this applies to non-visual difficulties in general (such as depression and OCD) people come to their own conclusions of the way people cope and suffer. When a man has a broken leg we can sympathise but when he has a mental illness or developmental disorder we can't actually see it so therefore are unable to visually see and understand his suffering accurately or as much. My point is, and I say this very warily, is it easier to cope with public stigmas better if a child has downs syndrome because of their facial features? I'm not saying downs is an easier condition to cope with than autism. That is NOT what I am saying. But I can't help but think if people new when they saw my sons they were autistic that, they would instinctually understand his difficulties better. I know I sound incredibly selfish and maybe I am but continually defending your child's behaviour is hard and you are continually on edge to prove your child is really suffering and has difficulties and isn't just naughty or a product of bad parenting.

Thursday.
Some days I really miss my brother Joseph. I wish he lived closer to us all. Although we did do a lot of falling out at one point but I'm sure that's all fine now. I'm very happy and secure with having such a big family and I feel very lucky. It's just a shame we don't see more of each other, we were a lot closer when we were younger.

Oh I wish I could climb into your head,

Alas I just stare and smile instead.

You're my muffin my cupcake my friend and inspiration,

*I'm proud to call you son,
my best blood relation.*

*Never go, never leave, you
make me complete,*

*Calling you my blessing is
my wonderful treat.*

Friday.

I don't deal with stress well especially when it is the result of someone I don't know very well. I get a kind of fight or flight thing going on, I either run and cry or stay and fight. Fight till the end. I won't let anyone get the better of me when I am in that state. But isn't everyone like this to some degree? I can't believe everything is down to my "condition". I have a real problem with criticism, my psychology degree taught me that this is because I was continuously criticised as a child. I would go with that. If I am criticised by strangers then I couldn't care less, but my family and friends I find it extremely hard to handle.

Saturday.
Today I went sledging with the kids. I absolutely loved it, having little boys is a wonderful excuse to be a kid and scream your head off in front of snotty mums.

Sunday.
I think this nation is obsessed with intelligence. Well for that matter, the world. Most people measure intelligence with academia but I believe it can be measured in many different ways. If we experienced nuclear warfare today it wouldn't be the people with a big IQ. The people who are used to been outdoors, who are physically strong and have good coordination would be far better. So the plumbers, sport people and builders could probably survive a lot longer. What's a psychology degree going to go for you when you need food, water and electricity?

Monday.
Why does everyone always want to give everyone else advice? Why do people believe they have enough infinite wisdom that they can change someone's life with a couple of

right on opinions and think life is just as black and white as that??? DEEEEEERRRRR!

Tuesday.
Today I feel completely hopeless and am on the verge of tears all day. My father in law has been very ill lately and its hit me harder than I ever thought it would. The last person to die in my family was my great great granddad Gaines in 1987. I've never really dealt with death and it scares the crap out of me. I need to be strong for Ben and the boys and make sure there feeling as good as they can. A little cry everyday has kept me going.

Wednesday.
I have decided that I need to approach the issue of death and illness in a very gradual way. I have no idea what I'm supposed to say. This is going to be one of those poignant memories my sons will always remember and I need to get it right.

Thursday.
Today we had the call from my father in-law, he was crying, I've never known him to cry and it makes me feel helpless. Anyway it's what we expected, lung cancer. We find out tomorrow if its spread and how serious it is. Ben and I have decided to ask Peter to come and live

with us while he's ill. I really don't want him living fifty miles away all alone when he needs so much care. I've decided if he wants to stay with us that Ben and I will sleep on a mattress in the room and he can have our room, he needs to be comfortable. I don't want him worrying about anything but recovery.

Friday.
Late last night Moses came down stairs crying. He had been watching the film "death becomes her" and was insistent that he wants to live for eternity. We had a long conversation about the fact that he won't die for at least sixty years because we have strong genes and his great great grandma is ninety two.

Saturday.
Well the cancer has spread to his brain and his stomach. He's been told he has to go be with his family. I immediately rang my brother Joseph as Ben was on his way home. He was amazing and very calm in his manner. He immediately made me feel at ease. Joseph said I am strong and ill get through this, it's true I will, but it's also true that caring for Peter is going to be harrowing and I don't truly no what I am taking on. We've asked him to come and live with us so we can care for him. His face just lit up and he was delighted. I know it's going to be difficult but I

know I can do it, but overall my priority is Ben and the kids. Ben's at college, soon at university. I suddenly feel strong and I know this feeling will last, because it has to. Joseph and I aren't particularly close but today he made me feel like he was really there for me and we were building bridges. Many years ago I upset him a lot and I'm very sorry for that, it was my entire fault. He knows this but I just wish we were closer.

Sunday.
Its 3:30am and I was woken up by my own crying. It's funny you know, you think your coping but then your brain just decides it has different ideas. It's as though it tells me that I'm coping too well and a breakdown is inevitable. Just keep going Emma, you have to for your family to get them through this.

Monday.
If I had a pound for every time I heard someone say "ohhh tha could write a book on mi life" I'd have, well at least £50. And I'd be forever be correcting peoples bad English. Well I really think you could write a book on mine. My father in-law is coming home to spend his last weeks with Ben and I in a few days. I can't wait to see him. I've ripped out the en suite and it will be done within a week. It's amazing how physically exhausted you become by been mentally drained.

I feel that way at the moment. I need to support Ben, but I fear I can't even care for myself.

Tuesday.

When you have a man dying in your family there are many emotions, delusion and anger within the home. This is often taken out on the kids and each other. Certainly not threw violence in this family but life isn't the same. Peter believes he's going to buy a new car and drive around like everything's normal. I would never want to take away of his independence or dignity but he has brain cancer and has had two fits within a week. By law he cannot drive or get insurance. He won't listen. What can we do?!

Wednesday.

Quiche made, ironing done, vacuuming done, tide mark removed from bath (well we might have a visitor) took mum to Primarni and every other shop in the shopping centre, I'm glad she has a disabled badge otherwise id need one my bloody self.

Thursday.

I bought all my tiles, bathroom sink, paint, taps and shower for the en suite, I can't bloody wait. Oh I also broke my thumb with a hammer as I accidently missed the chisel trying to get the tiles off. I gave up in the end. Well, midsummer murders were on!

Friday.
What if I want to go to bed? I mean I have to sleep in the room and if I'm tired I can't escape. If I'm tired it makes me cry, my chronic fatigue is down to my glandular fever as an adult. It's crippling and can affect you for the rest of your life. PATHETIC I here you scream. Whilst waving around your Claire Sweeny jazz hands! I'm selfish, I know I am, but I know my limits. Am I selfish? Or am I bipolar? Or is that just my mood today? Or should I just blame it on the meds. Selfish? Meds? Selfish? Meds? Anyway I'm feeling creative, I suppose that means I'm going high and my wit will return. Here comes the cleaning, talking incessantly, rambling and spewing verbal crap whilst my brain goes faster than my gob. Happy days?

Saturday.
I cannot imagine the day I have to tell Moses his granddad spider has died. Talking to children about dying brings almost as many questions as the sex talk does and I'm not even onto that yet. He's so sensitive but I've decided to go down the religious route. Even though I'm not religious I just want him to feel as clear and content about the situation as he can.

Stop trying to tell me how to live my life,

The path I take is mine you opinionated lowlife.

Ever herd of "he who casts the first stone"?

People like you must feel extremely alone.

My life is mine, my decisions are right for me,

I'm happy, I am successful just watch you will see.

Your opinions are futile, useless and juvenile,

I smile all day long

Welcome home Peter.

Sunday. So today's the day, kids are at Ben's mums and our mattress is in the conservatory and all clothes packed away. The house has been bleached within an inch of its life and I have a continua's feeling that I'm not doing enough. That's me by nature I think.

The journey took about two hours there and two hours back. Plus two hours to empty Peter bungalow and then only an hour to unload his things in his room. At five 5pm we could see how tired he was, continuously coughing up sputum and groaning when he walked. After ten minutes he made it up the stairs to bed with the help from Ben. He stayed up there until 8am. Poor guy, he was exhausted. Mind you we all were.

I was worried about Ben a lot today as he deals with a lot and although I just moan about what's bothering me, he just stays quiet until he rarely cracks. Anyway, when we dropped the kids off at Ben's mums she shouted (as we were just getting into the car) "don't worry, I'll go in a home, I won't be a burden to anybody"! Ben was in that much shock at her vile comment he just drove off. He was really upset and later spoke to her at which she denied all knowledge.

Fuck her; she certainly will be put in her home, well unless she agrees to euthanasia.

Monday.
Today Ben has a maths exam and can't miss it. I have an appointment with my psychiatrist at one and I defiantly can't miss that, my mental health is suffering severely and I'm very conscious my bodies trying to have a bipolar high, I don't have time for that. So Peter will have to be here for an hour or so by himself. It's unavoidable at the moment.

Tuesday.
So, today I have blagged a shit load of clothes from my brothers. Harrys trousers are hanging off of him and as my brothers are like tall bean poles I thought its better than a trip to

Primarni. He can't even make it to the wardrobe let alone a clothes shop.

Wednesday.

I hate blood tests, smears, the dentist and Botox and like a wimp I pop a Valium each time. I know that's not good. But it's rare and it works for me. Anyway I had my three monthly lithium and thyroid bloods taken today. My worst fear happened and it was a new nurse. She put the needle in four times and I told her not again. She called in the doctor. What did he do? Snap off the needle in my arm. There was blood everywhere and I screamed the place down. Anyway after a few minutes I left, calmed down and was greeted by a giggling group of patients in the waiting room. I swear even the fish where staring.

Thursday.

Today a nurse came from Macmillan. She was wonderful and truly was such an inspirational woman. She explained how Peter will deteriorate eventually and what we should expect and when to contact them and the Red Cross. Mainly for reasons of bodily function loss and signs of deterioration. I don't want to get to that point but we need to be prepared. But can anyone be that prepared?!

Friday.
Today we were told we could have a wheel chair for Peter. A mobility scooter will be better but for now this will mean we can get him out and about in the fresh air, maybe even take him to the local water park and have some lunch.

Saturday.
I really believe that Noah is dyslexic. The problem is I have heard from so many other parents that school will not pay for a dyslexia assessment. So I have to pay three hundred pounds to get him help. Just another typical example of having to fight and pay to get the correct help for children with disabilities.

Sunday.
I'm a cook; I cook a huge amount, and bake. But recently I've come across "so juicy" you stick your ribs, chicken or beef in a bag and sprinkle over the powder to create a delectable meal for all the family. Pah, nah I'm just a lazy arse that can't be bothered with Sunday dinner.

Monday.
Today was my psychiatry appointment and I had to go see him at a nice private hospital I can't afford in the centre of Leeds. He's been a great adviser for me and really helped with my medication. Today I was sad because of all the recent upheaval;

surprisingly he said I was rather focused, even though I was very upset. I feel as though I'm not doing enough for everyone. But Dr Wong explained that I'm not going high, I'm just going through what everyone else would normally experience when their nursing a dying man. I'm focused, sad but determined and that's all at the moment I can ask for. But what will tomorrow bring?

Tuesday.
Big shop today. My word, the list is a mile long. I actually look forward to my weekly shop. I know that sounds sad but it's time to myself on my own, slow pace and buying nice girly crap I don't need. Like candles, air fresheners, orchids, or daffodils if it's a skinny week. Daffs are actually my favourite flowers and are all over my garden and house. Wish my hay fever took a week off.

Wednesday.
I buy Easter eggs every other week. I eat Easter eggs every other week. Peter sleeps all day. I mean probably twenty out of the twenty four hours in the day. He wears a hat and a fleece around his neck as he seems to be always cold at the top of his body. I don't know what this means but it seems to be helping him.

Thursday.

I have never met a more inspiring man. A man who is so full of hope and life, is it hope? Or does he just not understand the magnitude of his illness? Age UK came today and we chatted for over an hour. It's funny, no one ever mentions death. Instead it's just the practical things of buying new clothes because he's lost weight and what time he has to take his medication.

I have been trying to get a blue badge for Peter for a few days now. Why do people make it so damn hard to make a dying man and his family's life just that little bit easier? I was passed around four times and was on hold for a total of an hour. In the end I informed the woman I originally stated with that "by the time I got any assistance the poor man would probably be dead!" and hung up. I probably shouldn't have said that but I got rather cocked off!

Maybe people who are dying and are older cope better because they know the people their leaving behind can cope because there all grown up. Younger people seem to have so much more responsibility. I'm at one of the most frightening times in my life, but yet I'm at one of my happiest.

We all seem to be coping; laughter really has been the best medicine today.

Friday.
I thought about my dad today. I mean my biological dad. He left when I was four and Joseph was two. I find as I get older he becomes more and more of a distance memory and of less importance I suppose. When I was younger I always imagined which part of my personality was from my mum and which from my dad. I suppose I'll never know.

But my only dad is my real dad. John.

Saturday.
Sometimes I get little obsessions. At the moment it's making sure the kids teeth are cleaned properly. But this means I actually have to do it for them. I hate the fact that they will ever have bad teeth, people judge you on that and I don't want that for them. The other is their homework, I find myself rather disappointed when they don't get house point and a "well done" on their work. Silly I know but because it's so hard to get them to sit, not cry and concentrate whilst doing the work, I feel disappointed when the hard work they both do isn't acknowledged. But I suppose they have a lot of work to mark.

Sunday. Moses just won't listen today. I just end up screaming at him. If I tell him to do something he just ignores what I say. I'm not the kind of mother to accept that. Give me a few weeks and ill condition that child to eat all his carrots just by the sound of a whistle. Today is a very frustrating day!

Monday. Today I woke up and thought. God Emma you look hot! I mean really nice, I don't mind admitting this as there is nothing wrong in taking pride in oneself. Anyway, it's given me a positive start to the day. Ben had what feels like his 100th exam today, it must be hard for him to concentrate. He's got into three universities now and onto five degrees. I'm so proud of him.

Tuesday. Why do I go shopping with my mum? I am determined not to spend. It can be Asda living, Primark, Sainsbury's or Debenhams and I always buy something. She's a bad influence on me.

Wednesday. I hate swimming because I'm so conscious of my body. I'm a size twelve, big boobs and an equally big arse. But today I plucked up enough courage to drag my saggy belly to the Morley baths. I did thirty one lengths and waited at the side while my friend finished her fifty lengths. I wonder if the water really does change blue if you pee in it. And why the hell is there always a grotty plaster? Some people!

Thursday.

Today's been a rather an up and down day. My mum's friend came and started on the en suite. He's great. A war veteran, who's only forty but has been in more than one war. He's training at university to be a councillor for ex-service men. How wonderful. I love how more and more people like him, me and so many others prove that no matter how your life begins you can achieve anything. And what's more, anything that's actually worth doing and extremely worthwhile. So, he opens up the shower and it's already had a small fire in it. I got a bit emotional as my cousin's shower set the house on fire only three weeks ago and the baby was trapped in the bedroom. So tomorrow a sparky is coming and fitting Peter's new shower so its super safe and I don't need to worry. Apart from the bill! I'm worried about it, I hate it when my bank balance gets below three hundred pounds and I owe money out. I suppose it's just feeling uncertain. Hopefully tomorrow will be a lot more positive. I can't wait for my day off Saturday from all the pressure of home. Is that selfish? Or is it more selfish to believe I'm supermom?!

8:30 at night and Peter took his first step on the stairs. Ben was up stairs and I'd put the telly on. He fell straight on his back and screamed and moaned. A scream from a dying very ill man is different to another man. It's deeper and sadder. He hurt his shoulder but mostly it's his pride that's hurt. Moses saw it happen and started to cry; I immediately ran to him and calmed him down, all Noah could say was "my tooth's come out my tooth's come out". Oh what a day, but tomorrows another start to a fresh new memory making machine.

Friday.
You can't heal a man just by loving him alone. He's so ill. He's frustrated and his hope is fading. I've read all about the signs that death is near but I honestly don't want to think about it. I just want to carry on loving this wonderful man and maybe he'll be here with us just that little bit longer. I really can't see us all going to see Peter's friends in Withernsea happening tomorrow. But how can you tell a seventy one year old man he can't do something. Respect plays a huge part in this progression.

Saturday.

Peter, Ben and the kids are off to Withernsea today. I'm quite relived as a day to myself is just what the doctor ordered. And what am I going to do with my day? Bugger all! Except sit on my fat arse watching scary movies all by myself. I am off to my mates nearby though so that will be good to have a conversation that isn't bloody morbid. I'm also going to watch a scary movie tonight all by myself. There was a time I wouldn't ever watch scary crap by myself. I'm a big girl now.

Sunday.

How can you tell a dying man to stop telling off my bloody kids? If you do not understand autism then don't shout at them every time they display an autistic symptom. I can't make Peter understand, and is it worth the aggravation anyway? And I can't make the kids understand because they are kids and their dealing with a huge amount. I feel like I can't leave the kids and I can't go in my own living room. I just want to cry. Writing this fucking diary isn't helping either, I need a bloody Valium. When Peters ill it's awful, but when he's chatty he's a pain in the arse. I know it sounds mean but if I can't be honest between me, my mind and

Microsoft word, then when the hell can I be honest?

Monday.
Since Peters been here I have felt really needed, like I have a purpose and a job to do. I clean all the time and do all my little jobs. Windows are cleaned and cupboards are organised. Dinner is prepared by four in the afternoon and I feel like I'm looking after my family. That makes me feel good.

Tuesday.
I spoke to Macmillan today as my auntie, who is also a doctor, advised me that we all need to get together and discuss the full extent of Peters illness. When I spoke to Macmillan she assured me that she was going to investigate the medical notes but more importantly she wanted to build a good relationship with Peter first before she got to the more serious issues. I completely understand that. He was tired today but he has pain in his stomach. I've felt as though I have wanted to be out of the house a lot today and just felt like my head was going to explode. I visited the doctor and my lithium levels are extremely low so I am going up to one gram. I was also given Valium. So let's see what tomorrow brings. Lunch with mummy and maybe a kip in the afternoon. Bliss.

Wednesday.
Had a great lunch with mum today. We had a little bitch and a trip around Asda buying shite. That was about it. Peter went to bed at five so Ben and I spent some time with the kids watching Harry hill as they think it's hysterical. I did feel a little guilty though as a friend of mine came to the door wanting to come in for a cup of tea but I was really stressed and said, more with my eyes than my face, that I wasn't up to it. I felt a bit bad. Am I selfish? Fuck knows I aren't a shrink.

Thursday.
Drilling, shouting, door knocking, slamming, phone ringing and appointments to be made. I am going bananas. But isn't it better to be busy rather than been bored and feeling useless. Ben has a bank appointment at half one about Peters life policies so it's a bit tense. Also age uk came this morning and she is just worth her salt. Had a nice chat and I can see she's worried because harries affairs, including his health are not been managed properly. Let's see what the bank will say, maybe good news.

Ben went to the bank with Peter. Basically he has two thousand pounds to bury him. That's not great but we'll cope with that when the time comes. The thing that's worrying us is that when the bank manager asked Peter what illness he had, Peter said "brain cancer, but its curable". As a family that lives with a man who is incredibly ill there is a certain amount of denial he goes through. And that's ok because that's his prerogative, his right and maybe it gives him hope. But Peter has been told he is going to die but he's regressing and solely believes he can be cured. It makes me cry but I have to hold it back and keep making the cups of tea and making his bed on a morning. All he tells us all the time is "I just want to be with my family". Well we can give him that.

Friday. Found out I need a new pump for the shower today. That's £150, I nearly cried but id saved a bit so we had enough and Greg, the plumber said he wouldn't charge me as it wasn't a big job. I hear he likes vodka so a bottle of Smirnoff will be in order. He's been fantastic.

Ben took the kids, Peter and Ben's sister Georgia to the pub tonight. Just for an hour. My children rarely go to the pub as I really hate kids in pubs. I think it stems from me and my two brothers going to our local in the next town every single day for years and years. I didn't want that for them.

Saturday.

I've painted my en suite today, just makes me feel like I'm getting somewhere as it's pretty slow. So I went and bough the paint and stopped at Aldi. Do you know they don't do carrier bags? I wish someone would have had bloody told me that! Everyone seems to be pissing me off at the moment, if Peter talks to me or Ben gets in my way I end up losing my rag and just walking away. I walk away a lot; I don't trust myself as I know what I am capable of if I lose it. We got a Chinese tonight and I am sat with Peter, I know it sounds mean but I just hope he goes to bed soon so I can relax. My mum rang me, she told me that her and my auntie Lily where off to get their Botox done one Wednesday. I told her I couldn't afford it but my mum immediately said "don't worry it's on me" I developed the biggest smile in Sainsbury's, and there was some right grumpy buggers in there.

Sunday.

Well its mother's day and I was woken at 4:30am, 6am and then 8am. I'm knackered but I got up and went to the park with the kids and Peter. I think all five of us enjoyed the fresh air and bloody needed it. I got some cards from the kids and then took mine to my mums. I stopped off at Tesco's and quite strangely they were selling every bouquet off with 75% off. Weird considering it was mother's day but I bought a massive bunch for my mum and my grandma too. They loved them, mum showed me around her half-done living room yet again telling me what she had done and what needed doing whilst my dad rolled his eyes. Rather too nineties show home for me but god is my mums house very clean and in order. My mum would have been great if she had been a housewife in the 1940s.

The rest of the day I was a bit moody, for some reason everyone was getting on my nerves. I had a kip and felt a bit better. I've been having some worries recently about how much I am eating. I'm at the local supermarket twice a day eating doughnuts and cheese straws, I'm kind of doing it in secret and hiding food and it's starting to worry me. When I was around fifteen, I did the same and I made myself sick until all my back teeth rotted. I don't know if its stress, the lithium or I am just a greedy bastard. But the problem with having bipolar is ill eat like a thirty stone, Greggs/jezza lover or I'll go the opposite was and start having a huge fear of food. I can't seem to do anything sensibly, it all has to be one extreme to another. Tomorrow I am going to try to eat hardly anything.

Families are amazing, helpful and loving.

But sometimes there fuckwits betray me and need a good shoving.

Is it me? Is it them?

But should I judge this much should I be the one to condemn.

Am I a far better friend and family member than those who make me sad?

Or do all these indulgent questions make me bad?

I love you mum so love me back,

How dare you shun me and make me feel like crap,

I am worthy of cuddles, smiles and what's up love?

Maybe the answers will not resolve themselves until where both above.

Monday. The problem with having a dying relative is that sometimes, and defiantly in my case, your friends can abandon you. Are they scared? Do they not know what to say? Or do they just not give a shit? I'll go for the latter because a text takes nothing. But my family, all five generations are there and have been truly amazing. Peter has been asking over and over if one of his daughters will contact him. Were in a very hard position because we know she doesn't want to. What are we supposed to say to a man who wants to talk one last time to his child that she doesn't want to know? We just have to distract him because we won't hurt him like that even if she will. I don't care what her pathetic reasons are, he's dying and she will regret this. Well if she was capable of normal emotions, like mother like daughter, two of a kind, I suppose you just have to pity that type of hollow individual. How sad.

Tuesday.

Had a hospital appointment today with my GP, she says I need to keep taking diazepam just to get me by, but as and when, not regularly. That works for me. So my mum, Auntie Lily and I went to see the woman who does our Botox and derma fillers. I felt great having a break and laughing with my family. The woman who does our Botox has had a mini facelift and she looks amazing. I'd be happy if I look half that good at her age.

Wednesday.

We were told by Georgia today that Rose (Peters other daughter) hasn't been to see Peter because she has a throat infection. Oh, do these pass over the phone? Has she had one for two years? Bullshit. She's a selfish cow and in all honesty I couldn't care less if they didn't get on when she was a kid. She lived with him into her thirty's and I also lived with them. The problem is that selfish bitch is too much like her selfish bitch of a mother. I suppose you just have to feel sorry for self-important people like this, if I disowned my mother for everything she did wrong against me I wouldn't have spoken to her from the age of eleven. Shit happens, she doesn't know what fucking suffering is, but if she ever wants to know I'll give her my fucking life story. Good god I have a potty mouth.

Thursday.
Today's been a pretty good day, apart from my face killing from the derma filler I had last night it's been pretty good. Georgia came up today (Ben's sister) and watched Peter for an hour while we went for lunch at the local. It's good, and very helpful to have these times, it helps Ben and I stay close and strong. Georgia and I had a little chat about Peter which was nice we haven't spoken in years and she told me shed come up at any time if we need a break so that's helpful. Still no word of Ben's other sister Rose. We keep been told different excuses as to why she has had no contact with Peter. She has to live with the fact that her father was dying and

asking for her and she would not, or couldn't come. I, Ben and Georgia will sleep well knowing we did everything we could.

Friday. I've been thinking a lot about our upcoming anniversary. We would have been married for fifteen years and I think it deserves a celebration. I have an idea; I have seen a lovely restaurant close by that my family wouldn't have been too before. I was thinking of taking sixteen relatives and Noah and Moses. Its fifteen pounds for a three course a la carte Sunday lunch and the menu looks lovely. Some of my relatives won't be invited and it's nothing personal but I can't afford to pay for everyone. Apart from Peter, none of Ben's relatives will be invited because apart from Peter and Georgia there just sour faced negative feeders, and this is a celebration, and it's going to be a great one. I hope where much closer to Georgia closer to the time, maybe bridges will be built and she and her husband can come too.

Saturday. Ben and Moses went fishing today. I thought it was a nice idea for Ben to spend some time away from home and college.

By the end of the day I felt resentful of being number one carer. Noah and I dropped Peter off at the local shopping centre and Georgia and her little girl Flora picked him up and they did a bit of shopping. We went back to get them a couple of hours later and Georgia came back and we looked threw a few old pictures. It was supposed to be a day off but in all honestly it was one of the hardest days wed had in the last three weeks.

Sunday.

I woke today in one of my more uncomfortable moods. I'm just scared of kicking off at anyone in my way, and I generally do. I feel like I can't go anywhere near Peter, he's irritating me and he doesn't even do anything wrong. Well, apart from repeating everything we say to the kids, when we're telling them off. Like his contribution will suddenly stop them from having autism and they'll become the perfect children. Well they already are.

Monday.

Ben and I are becoming very concerned about Peters mental health. He's talking about getting a loan; he believes he can do this because he has loan protection. He refuses to stop paying into a life policy that won't pay out until he's been paying into it for two years. He won't live two years but we can't kick his hope in the arse so the only thing we can do is let him throw his money away. He repeats himself over and over so I decided to ring Lynn, who is our allocated Sue Ryder worker. A bit like the work of Macmillan staff. She's wonderful and agrees with us that she needs to see him more regular and build up a closer relationship with him. The other thing we need to talk about is the trial. Peter has decided to do a cancer trial. I don't actually no why he's doing it. I've read the whole research and it has horrendous results. In fact it doesn't actually have results. If they don't get enough people on the research it will be "killed" there word, not mine. If I had terminal cancel, would I do the radiotherapy and the drug trial? Probably But from the outside looking in, its madness but it isn't my choice, it's his and he has to do what's right for him. At some point there is only hope left and I will endeavour to give him hope as much as I can. So, Lynn came round and just pretended she had to drop in for a form signing. We spoke about the trial and I got a bit upset. I don't want Peter to be just been seen as a number, he's a human being with a lot of love around him. Someone's daddy, granddad, father in-law and friend. We all had a good talk and felt much better afterwards. The sun beating on our backs in our deck chairs on the drive made life feel so much more positive. I feel better. I think Peter does too.

Tuesday.

Today I decided it was about time I did something for my favourite charity, The National Autistic Society. I've sent twenty two emails to companies to ask if they would donate ingredients for a bun sale. I love baking and I'm sure the local head master at the kid's school would let me do it there. The local nurses where supposed to come today but I didn't happen, we don't really need them yet though so it's not an issue.

We were told by the school today that Moses is been bullied. They wouldn't tell us by who but the night terrors inform us of that. Moses is insistent that he wants no-one to no he has autism so his teacher and I have decide that Moses will be removed from the class for half an hour and the children will be in formed, in the autism official manner (Ziggy) that Moses has a general diagnosis and he has certain difficulties and that's why he receives extra help and has certain difficulties. The word autism will not be mentioned. I also believe that parents need to be made aware that there is a child in that year with the condition and their children should try to understand that all people are different and a little bit of understanding is of great importance to the child who is having problems. It remains to be seen if this will happen but I won't hold my breath

Wednesday.
Its Ben's day off of college and I don't really know what to do with myself. I've been suffering from hay fever quite a lot but that's not surprising since I have been in the garden planting so much. I had a cuppa at my neighbour's Lulu's house and then went back to bed as I feel just, well, shagged! I woke up at twelve and forced myself to put some makeup on and a nice summery dress as it's so bloody warm. On the news there talking about fuel shortages, water shortages and food shortages. Good god it Armageddon. Well you know what, we'll survive. Why? Because where bloody British that's why and if this is the only crap thrown at us this year well I can't wait. I went to see my mum to drop off some Easter eggs for the family; I was met by my dad who took me next door to the neighbours. I think his speech is that bad now he won't even grunt or point. I love him so bloody much. Two daddy's poorly, two daddy's a shadow of their former selves. I pray you no. I pray every night, for my whole family (I'm a crap agnostic) to just keep going, just a little longer. I went into see

my mum and she was decorating the neighbour's bedroom while she's in rest bite getting her strength up. I know mum loves helping people but she's very selective. Now shed lend me money because that's how she shows her love, but if I asked for help painting my fence? I don't think so. One day she will need my help as she's only fifty two but her backs a mess. That will be uncomfortable, but I love her and maybe we'll become closer. Why am I waiting for my mum to get ill so I can get close to her, what the hell am I talking about? Anyway I got a call from school and Moses has been sent home as he had been sick and I actually believe it was genuine this time. Noah was excited and shuck Moses's hand for getting him out of school and hour early. Hmmm, partners in crime?

Thursday.

Peter had been sat in his chair on the drive in the sun today. He stood up to come in and Moses was coming down the stairs. As he grabbed his rail his foot slipped and I caught him. Moses got scared and Peter seemed to be stuck with his legs bent. He kept saying sorry but the last thing that man ever has to say to me is sorry. I held him for a moment and he regained his strength and sat in his comfy sofa spot for a rest. I made Sheppard's pie while Ben was doing the after school Warhammer club and it went down really well, so today was good. Oh I had a go in Peter's wheel chair, which was fun. My garden is just full of flowers, I think my obsession with gardening at the moment, beats baking I suppose. I have dozens of daffodils, tulips and well many miscellaneous. I'm buying some strawberry plants tomorrow and I'll be looking for a nice bench for Peter to sit on in the back garden.

Friday.
I have a meeting with the head today to ask if he would mention me in his newsletter for my charity bun sale. He rang me later and was very positive and agreed to the bun sale and to mention it in the newsletter. I got my first two positive replies from two supermarkets. Today Peter had an appointment regarding the cancer trial. Peter came home today from the hospital and has been told he meets the criteria to be involved in the research. This means he starts his radiotherapy in a week. I hope his side effects are not too bad but I think there that desperate to get anyone on the research they would have taken him anyway. I just want him to be treated well and not like a number.

Saturday.

I felt great this morning, like I had a lot of energy. Minds you that might have something to do with the fact that I'd just taken two co-codomol and wow do they open your eyes. But I am having horrible issues with my shoulder and back. Peter had a call today from a man wanting to buy his caravan. He's been offered six thousand which is great for him. He's offered us a thousand pounds for the en-suite and gas bill but I feel incredibly uncomfortable about him giving us the money. I think he feels just as uncomfortable so we declined. Anyway after I pay off my mum the money we owe her and the gas bill well won't be left with anything but life will be a lot easier. They've all just gone up to my mums for Noah and Moses's pocket money. There really excited and they want to go to toys r us. I think children believe ten pounds buys the earth. I think I'll do the whole, "dine in for two" from M&S for Ben and I tonight. As soon as where alone I really need to try and spend some time with him.

Sunday.

Today was horrible. I've got to a point where I actually think I hate me mother. No, really! My mum has told so many lies and especially about me I couldn't even write them all down. Today I found out that she had told my grandmother that I am bankrupt. What a crock. That's just completely untrue. My mum had been really rude to my granddad because he had bought my cousin a new mattress and accused him of doing more for her sister, my auntie. My grandma was really upset about this and kept trying to give me money. I continually said no but eventually took fifty pounds and said I would give it to my mum as I still owed her money from my new en-suite, I felt like shit. My brother Luke had taken me, mum and my dad to a local for lunch today and it was nice but later speaking to my grandma and hearing all she said about my mum I got to a point where I just couldn't stop crying. Ben's of to fit a curtain rail at my mums tomorrow so I hope to god he doesn't get funny with her. I'm getting to the point where I am going to really lose it with my mum, and if that happens we will never speak again. There's only so much brushing off of the situation you can do and I am only human.

Monday.
It's the Easter holidays and where all at home. It's fine at the moment but I can imagine my patience is going to wear thin very soon. I taught Moses how to play Jim rummy and black jack today. My word that child learns

quickly. I have literally played fifteen times today. Peter also gave Moses his laptop today. This has been one of those times where I have noticed my son has been truly grateful for something and felt very lucky. I felt rather proud of him.

Tuesday.

What a crappy day. For two reasons, well the first reason I don't actually understand. It's when you feel down but you don't actually know why. I hate been like that because there's no solution. If I knew what was wrong I could attempt to solve it. I suppose with everything going on I am just a bit down. The second was when I got home and found I was no longer on my grandmas neighbours face book and I couldn't understand why. I asked my auntie and she told me it was probably because sometimes I write really dramatic statuses. I said "do I "? And she replied "yes, didn't you no"? I explained "no, Lily, I didn't"? And I said goodbye. I then just deactivated my Facebook account. Not because of what she said because I think it's nonsense but I am sick of constantly checking it and I have realised it kind of controls a small part of my life. I think phones are doing that more and more, it creeps up on you, texting, BBM, Facebook, Twitter, apps, gps, gprs. I don't even know what half of these things are. I know it's only Facebook but I quite like my grandma's neighbour.

Wednesday.

Well I have been gardening for a full week and my garden was looking great, what happens? Bloody snow!

Peter starts his radiotherapy today. He's actually really excited, god I hope it goes well for him. He was given two month to live and he's already planning what he wants for Christmas. Georgia was up yesterday with Flora, it's amazing the difference it makes in picking up his spirits. I only wish his other daughter would visit him, for him, not anyone else. She's a hideous human being but he loves her and it would make his week. But Ben and I have agreed to drop it; it's her issue, not ours. I feel really down today. I just want to go to sleep and start all over again tomorrow. Lily hit a nerve. People tell me all the time that I'm going through a really bad time and I kind of just ignore it and get on with it. But if she believes I am moaning about it on face book, which I am not, I feel sick. The only things I have mentioned are the autism bun sale and if she's complaining about that then fuck her. If she can't understand how important it is to me then she's an idiot. That woman has never done anything worthwhile in her life!

Thursday.
Today Peter had his second day of radiotherapy. He's been a bit tired and his feet are swollen but apart from that he's doing great which is brilliant. Moses and I had one of our "chats" today about Noah and people knowing about him been autistic. He surprises me sometimes at how mature he is.

Friday.
I got talking to my neighbour today and she told me about her mum and that she's quite ill. I could see she was emotional and told me all about her. She offered for me to go out with her one night. I said I may do but to be honest I am more likely to come round if I needed a cry and laughed, but we had a giggle and I felt a bit better. It's amazing the people who come out of the woodwork and offer you a shoulder to cry on when you need one. It's also amazing who just abandons you.

Saturday.
Today Joseph and Millie came up with Milo. He's such a big boy now and he loved the cars Noah and Moses gave too him. It was nice to see them all and Milo really took to

Peter. I've been really tired today and I keep thinking I am getting down because I just can't stand been in the house, I feel like I just want to run away. My neighbour stopped me and asked how Peter was and how I was too. It's always nice when people ask how Ben and I are as sometimes I think people forget about the careers. When a tragedy like terminal cancer happens a strange thing happens. "Friends" make excuses and leave you or don't reply to your calls. Others that you may not have expected speak to you and offer help and a version of their experiences. People have offered help and I no its bullshit because it's just something people say, but others have truly meant it. I can see it in their eyes, the welling up of tears because they can feel your pain.

Sunday. Easter Sunday. Ben and I have got to have some time to ourselves today as I am really missing him, even though I am with him all the time. So, this morning Ben, I and the kids are going for a walk with the dog to the park and really just spend time as a family. I know it sounds like where leaving Peter out but we really do need time alone. At lunchtime Ben and I are dropping the kids at Ben's mums and where going for lunch. Although where certainly not

telling her that, as she wouldn't babysit if she knew it was for us. I know she'll ask what where doing because she's incredibly nosey but we'll make something up. He he.

Why do I run? Why do I care?

Why am I so overrun with despair?

I need my sanctuary, my den and my space,

There's just too much of this situation I cannot face.

My little room helps me breath,

I feel at home in my home,

I don't need to worry, cry or be alone.

I dare not cry, be selfish or moan,

I say over and over again that I am lucky, how dare I complain and retreat to my zone.

Help me be perfect, best mum, best carer, best daughter and wife,

Please, please help me suss out this complex life.

Do I moan too much? Is this just, well, life?

At the end of the day I may just be the world's worse complying lowlife.

Monday.
When will it end? I am truly hideous for thinking this I know. I am selfish and I hate change. I want my bedroom back, it's my safe place but it's not mine anymore. I'm disgusted that I get annoyed because all he wants to do is spend his thousands on crap and shite. Satellites' and cars he will never drive. But who's going to bury him? I know he should live for now and have fun and not worry about the inevitable end but we can't be left with a man to bury and no money. I know I said we would care for him and we will, and even though he offers us money all the time there is no way we would ever take a penny. Today's a sad and selfish day. God lord let me be a better person tomorrow.

Tuesday.
I played chess with Moses today. He cottoned on to the fact that I wanted to lose because he was taking so long and cheating.

Eventually I let him win and I won him at rummy three times. He hates losing but wow is he getting good. I was supposed to go to an appointment for Moses today but I forgot because it's been so hectic around the house with housework and in the garden. The garden looks lovely. Today was better and I am visiting my friend tomorrow so I am looking forward to that.

Wednesday.

Sometimes I just find myself staring, you no just looking at them. I stare and stare. I find myself just cupping them and touching them over and over. The coldness of the top of them and the overspill threw my fingers. There just bloody great.

Until I take my bra off!

Thursday.

Guess what? For I change, I've been really down today. But today I was told that my friend wouldn't be able to meet me tomorrow as she has something to do. I don't know if it's the change of plan that upsets me so much or the fact that Ben is going to the coast with the kids Peter, Georgia and Flora and the bloody dog and there's no room for me. I feel sorry for myself and guilty that I won't be walking on the sandy beach with my kids. Maybe a day to myself will do me good. Who am I kidding? Even I'm getting sick of my complying. I bought a big black shabby chic plaque today. It says "happiness is not a destination. It is a way of life"

Friday.

I've been on my own today and I have really enjoyed it. I like my own company, well most of the time; I always get a good conversation out of myself. Sometimes I can just get on with all the "things of the moment" things. I did loads of gardening today and ordered some sweet little herb signs. But on the other hand it gave me time to think and that's not always a good thing. I was convinced I was starting to develop depression today; if I am honest I have been thinking this for a while now. I'll be visiting my psychiatrist soon, I know I can't go on anti-depressants as they can make me high but we'll see what the quack has to say.

Saturday.

Shopping! Yeah. My weight is shooting up; I am looking forward to ordering my treadmill on Tuesday. I know it going to really get me motivated to stay in shape.

I'm sat here watching only fools and horses when I really want to watch "the voice" well I say I want to watch it, it's the lesser of two shite evils on a

Saturday night. Ben's out shooting with one of his friends and I am sat with Peter listening to him snore his head off. I slept really badly last night and my back is really hurting me. Ben told his dad this and asked him to have an early night. Its nine forty five and I'm almost crying. If he's tired why can't he just go to bloody bed? My bedroom is the living room. If he's awake, I am awake! Anyway I had a chat with my auntie Lynn today at my grandmothers. I was asking what to do when Peter dies. Apparently if he dies in bed I have to call the doctor and get a death certificate to be able to send him to a funeral director. I never knew this; I always thought you called an ambulance. I feel a bit naive now.

Sunday.
Peters finally sold his caravan. Ben has approached the issue of putting a bit away, he means for his funeral but it's such a delicate subject it needs to be dealt with properly. We've decided to involve the Sue Ryder group. If Peter died tomorrow we would have no control over his finances to bury him, the money would be under a solicitor and family issues would be rife. I just hope it can be organised, but why and how can we ask a dying man to organise his own funeral and finances? We can't.

Monday.

Today's been ok but after a rather uneventful day, Moses came home and had one screaming tantrum after another. Ben and I both tried to diffuse each issue he had but it gets to the point where he just needs to be removed from the situation. That's his bedroom. The problem is he just goes in there and destroys everything. For the second week he snapped his glasses. I had to get the laptop and television before they landed at the bottom of the stairs. He ended up with books in his room and nothing else. I feel for Peter as he really needs peace and quiet and I don't know how the situation will work when he really is on his death bed but I'm going to have to make a conscious decision to help Moses understand Peter's problems without upsetting him.

Tuesday.

It was a sad day today. Not only because I am feeling so incredibly down but the sue Ryder lady came to our house today. We spoke to Peter about power of attorney and his will. His body language became rather uncomfortable but we really have to organise this so there are no disruptions or misunderstandings when he passes. At one point Ben pointed out that Peter had always wished his finances where split three ways, Peter said well, "yes I did at one point but this may of changed". Oh god the dread is just pumping threw my veins.

Wednesday.

Ben wasn't at college today so we decided to go out and get some supplies for the garden. We both dug up the corner of the garden where the grass doesn't grow and laid down the weed cover and wood chips and our new bench on top. I'm hoping that flowers I have planted around it will grow around it and it will be a nice place for Peter to sit in the sun. Later we went to a local carvery for some lunch. It was a good day I think, I bit of "Ben and I time".

Thursday.

I feel like I'm coming out of my down patch. I'm starting to be able to deal with daily tasks a lot easier. Ben was at college all day and I kept nipping out just to have a breather, not that Peters a burden, I just need a bit of space sometimes. Tonight there was a program on the television about Autism by Louis Theroux. My brother Joseph posted the link on my Facebook page and wrote the following about me, "Every day I feel blessed for my little boy and my nephews knowing that they are all special in their unique way. My sister is one of the strongest people I know x". It made me cry, it was a lovely thing to say.

Friday.
Peter and I watched a comedy today, it was lovely to watch him laugh and forget about the cancer for a short time. I've known this man for eighteen years and he's such an easy man to love. I gave him a big kiss on his bald head before he went to bed tonight. Love you Peter.

Saturday.
Today we went to the national railway museum. It's somewhere we used to take the kids years ago and they would get so excited. We hadn't gone for a couple of years and thought it would be a great idea to take Peter too. The morning went smoothly and I always get excited seeing the trains, I feel like a kid. Anything big and noisy gets me all childish and smiley. On the way home we stopped at McDonalds and I had a salad. Which, in all honesty, had as many calories in it as a Big Mac. So what was the point of that? Peter seems in good spirits although it's obvious his mobility isn't improving. I feel at the moment that I am coping well but Moses is having real issues with his hyperactivity. He won't stop screaming and he won't stop been even

more demanding than usual. It's hard. I hate saying that but keeping everyone happy is hard.

Sunday. Peter woke this morning in a lot of pain. His back is getting worse, the calls have been made and now where just waiting for the GP.

Peter went in, it looks like his MRI scan has been brought forward.

The beginning of the end.

Monday. Today Ben and Georgia went to visit Peter in hospital, he didn't look well and I think Bens concerns are really growing for him. When Ben got home we had a chat about Rose. Georgia had spent the weekend with Rose and it had been made quite clear that Rose would not be seeing her father again, at all. I think in some way it was a relief for all of us. Not that she wasn't going to come, but more so that we had a definite no, the question was, do we tell Peter? We had a long chat and decided that we would, but not on the same day as the will, which is Wednesday and just to tell Peter that it was very unlikely she would be coming. People could think well why say anything? Peter asks about her, just as Georgia is stuck between Ben and Rose, we are stuck between Peter and Rose. I will not lie to him.

Tuesday.
Today has been rather hectic and its only noon. I had to see Moses's psychiatrist this morning because of his hyperactive behaviour and his violent streaks. I was adamant that I didn't want his medication increased but at the end of the hour long meeting we agreed that if he had had a bad school day he could take a 10mg tablet after school. I was happy with this. When I got home I had a couple of hours to get myself sorted and pick up a couple of prescriptions. Millie called me and told me they were up and I could go see Milo at my mum's house. All of a sudden I burst into tears, I don't know why. Sometimes I just don't realise how much I am dealing with. We had a chat and she made me feel better. Ben called me and told me his dad rang him and asked to see him this afternoon and to see George? We don't know who this is and Peter was very vague. I hope it isn't bad news but Ben will be speaking to his dad about Rose today and informing him she won't be coming. I hope Ben approaches this sensitively.

Ben isn't telling tales, but Peter mentions Rose and it's cruel to let Peter have the hope of her coming to see him. There is hope. And then there's delusion. We love him and he will be ok.

Ben visited Peter and its apparent that the cancer is in his spine and also his spinal fluid so its continually going up and down his brain. The doctor advised Ben that this was the beginning of the end and six weeks was probably the time Peter has left. A time span is horrible to contemplate. Ben had a discussion with his father about Rose. He told him it would be very unlikely that Rose will be visiting him. Peter started to cry and then so did Ben. I can't imagine how sad that must have been. Ben has a new hatred for Rose that I've never seen him have with anyone. Ben called Georgia and she was sad for her dad and agreed it was a bloody mess. He also called his mum, all we hear from her is "Rose has her reasons". We also found out that Peter had visited Rose on a number of occasions and she was in, but refused to answer the door. I can't explain how sad that is. The impression seems to be that Peter may have done something wrong. I don't know if that is true but my dad left me at four years old and never came home again. What Peter did was look after his three children when their mother left them behind. Still I suppose you never know what goes on in relationships. But knowing what I do about Rose? Probably some blown out of proportion dramatic bullshit!

Wednesday.

Peters coming home from the hospital today and I am just waiting for him now. He's had his shot of radiotherapy and is been sent home with morphine. A solicitor visited him at the hospital to devise his will. As soon as he came out Millie, the solicitor asked if he was happy, Peter said he was. He also said, "Oh I have left Rose out". Ben really didn't want to know that.

When Peter arrived home he fell straight asleep on the sofa, hearing his heavy breathing wasn't irritating anymore, but reassuring instead. Ben and Peter had been waiting five and a half hours at the hospital pharmacy for his morphine. In the end they just left as Ben had a dental appointment he had been waiting three months for. It's a disgraceful example of our NHS People with terminal cancer shouldn't be treated like that. No wonder there are so many posters in hospitals regarding abuse to hospital staff, if I was there I would have most certainly kicked off.

Thursday.

Peter has had a great day today. His mood has lifted considerably and he's walking around like a strong nimble twenty one year old. Everyone keeps saying to me "he will go really quick Emma, you won't see it coming!) Bullshit I won't.

Friday.

Ben and I lay on our oversized squashy mattress in our living room in a semi sleep state. I heard a noise over and over. A shout but combined with a moan too. Ben shot up and yelled "it's my dad". He ran upstairs and I followed, half way up I realised I was naked so immediately ran back down. Peter couldn't breathe; he was panicking because he couldn't get out of bed to go to the bathroom. The ambulance arrived and was met by Peter propped up by pillows; Ben was sat with a big smile on his face and only his pants on. "I bet you've seen it all before?", have to see the funny side I suppose. Peter was stabilised but it was obvious there was more wrong than a panic attack. When he got to the hospital it was said that the lung he didn't have cancer in had pneumonia in it. Ben and Georgia where advised that only fifty per cent of healthy adult survive the condition. I really didn't realise the illness was that serious. He was put on antibiotics but told that if there was no improvement in forty eight hours then they would just make him comfortable. I went to the hospital and sat with Ben and Georgia for a few hours, it was emotional. The normal texts where sent to Rose but there was no reply. He was very nearly on his death bed and she didn't come. I have great pity for a woman like that, but I suppose living with who she is punishment enough. That's not a dig, it's actually true. We settled him in and Ben visited later and he seemed a bit perkier. Hectic day but he's getting the help he needs.

Saturday.
Peter seemed a lot more upbeat this morning, I have no idea how my husband copes so well. Maybe it's because he's had to put up with all my shit for so many years, maybe he's immune to stress.

Sunday.
Today's been ok, I have had a good clean around and the kids and I made homemade pizzas. At six this evening Ben and Georgia got a call from the hospital to come in as Peters in a bit of distress. I hope it's nothing but it sounded bad.

Its ten pm and I am just sat staring at the four walls, waiting for news, any news. Ben told me the antibiotics have been stopped as there not working and it was time to make him comfortable. I think that's a nice way of saying drug him up and let him die in his own time. Ben just lost it at that point. I feel retched.

Ben arrived home at half past one am. Peter passed away. I cuddled my man and we cried together until we fell asleep on our mattress in each other's arms in the living room. Today's a sad day. And it hasn't even started yet.

Monday.

I cannot believe how much we have done today. We have decided not to tell the children until the weekend, we don't want to upset Moses before his trip to Whitby with school and Ben really wants to go with him. We had to wait until ten to call for the death certificate from the hospital. Of course the doctors were busy so it wasn't until three that we got it. Ben, myself, Georgia and her husband Thomas all went to the funeral director and sat in a little room and were met by a lovely lady who was so helpful. Georgia and I got a bit emotional but the process didn't take long. The coffin will have a union jack on it from the prison, as he was a prison officer and the cars will leave from our house. The only down fall was the deposit of over nine hundred pounds they wanted. So Georgia and I paid half each. I'm officially skint but well worth it. Rose has been informed. No reply.

Tuesday.
Today I heard my phone ring. When I saw it was my grandmother I knew she would be emotional. I picked it up and she just burst into tears and told me how upset she was, the thing is I love my grandma so very much but when I'm trying to keep things together she just set me off. I just fell to pieces. Tomorrow Ben and Moses are going away to Whitby on a school trip and Georgia and I are registering the death. I'm going to miss them so much, especially as this is an awful week. I'm just glad we've been able to protect the kids from it, until Friday anyway.

Wednesday.
This morning went quite smoothly considering so much was happening. I didn't go up to school because I had so much preparation to do at home for the town hall, petrol in car, shower, walk dog, clean up..........................take a breath, have I had my morning pee?. At twelve o'clock I picked up Georgia and Thomas and we drove just down the road to the town hall. When a person passes you

learn a lot very quickly about the ins and outs of what needs to be done. We registered the death (four quid a bloody copy!) but the cause of death said lung cancer, although it wasn't, it was pneumonia. Some people may think that well he did have lung cancer, but the fact is pneumonia took his life. If it wasn't for that he would still be here. We chose to accept it as we had other things to worry about. As we came out Thomas went to the toilet and I told Georgia how I thought Thomas was a really nice man and she smiled and said thanks but looked slightly confused. I explained that because Ben and I had always been given a negative view of him, and many others for that matter, but I was really glad Ben and I had got to know him properly. I felt better with myself telling her this as there has always been a strained relationship between us. But all in all this was down to Bens mum. A very sad and obviously spiteful woman with nothing better to do that play her kids off against each other. At night I tuck my children up in bed with their teddies and tell them I love them and know I have always done my best. I imagine she sits in a swivel chair stroking a big fluffy white cat plotting on how to make even more people hate her. You're not far off love, you keep going!

After picking up Noah from school my mum and I took him to pizza hut. Whenever one of the kids goes on a trip my mum insists we take the other one out. There seems to be a trend with grandparents insisting on feeding kids to show their love. And generally shite!

Thursday.
I took Noah to school this morning with no fuss. He's really excited that it's his cousin's milos birthday today at grandma's house and he's having a picnic tea with cake. I stopped off on my way home at my friends Lulu house. It was nice to have a chat with a friend as it feels like so many have just dwindled away since I've needed support. I suppose I found out who my friends were. We had a tea and a chat and I felt a bit better. Thursday for me was just cleaning and a whole lot of Jeremy Kyle, the Wright Stuff, and Maury, Steve Wilko and Bobs Burgers, diet coke and an hour on treadmill. Well I am not been a lazy arse if I watch crap TV on the treadmill am I?!

The tea party was nice and Milo loved his present. I love these family moments. It was obvious my heart wasn't in it and I am really missing Ben but it cheered me up a bit. I'm not looking forward to pulling that mattress through again.

Friday. I've felt really on edge today. I visited my mum and we visited the shops but I have just been desperate to see Ben. I've missed him so much. As soon as I saw him getting off the coach I gave him a huge hug. I almost forgot about Moses, but he reminded me to be a cool mum and not cuddle him. Ben said it was a lot of hard work with Moses and I can imagine. Moses's made a friend at school. A little girl called poppy. Ben says she's a lot like Moses and they get on great together. That makes me smile. That night Ben and I slept in the room and ate antipasti together. Today was a good day.

Saturday. This morning we decided to tell the children about their granddad. I guessed how each of them would react and I was right. Noah said "oh ok" and went to play on the Wii and Moses cried so we had a long chat and lots of cuddles.

Sunday. I visited my grandmother as this is where I always go when I need a cuddle. We had a little cry together and a cup of tea and I felt a little better. When I got home I got back into my pyjamas and started Sunday lunch. Slow roast pork shoulder, mash, Yorkshires, roast potatoes, veg and gravy. Mmmmmm.

Monday. Bank holiday and it feels like I can't actually get anything productive done until the funeral is over. It's always the same with me, it seems I can only manage one thing at a time and lose the plot if I have to cope with more than one major occurrence at a time. That's probably why I only have an automatic licence because I can't cope with the complex clutch, accelerator, mirrors brake nonsense you have to endure in a manual car. Does an automatic have a clutch? What's a clutch? One thing for is for sure, I never want to meet one. My idea of multi-tasking is looking at the view whilst scratching my arse at the same time.

Tuesday. Apparently whenever there is a bank holiday, the council also take off Tuesdays too. This is why we couldn't have the funeral today as there is no one to light the fire. The fire for the cremation! I don't really like how I put that.

Wednesday.

If you could ever describe a funeral and beautiful, that's how I would describe Peters send off. The sun was out and the cars arrived a bit early in mind of the traffic. No sign of Rose or best wishes from Ben's mum but Ben and I are realist and don't believe in miracles.

The coffin was covered in a beautiful union jack and the flowers where white with a royal blue back ground spelt out with the word dad. We got into the limonene and went slowly off from the estate. The cars made their way to the prison where he worked and when we arrived the emotion was overwhelming. The flag was at half-mast and around forty staff where lined up. The car stopped and the National Guard did his bit. I'll be honest I didn't quite understand what he was saying but all four of us fought back the tears and it really was wonderful. Watching the Hearst in front of our car and seeing the words "dad" made me realise how truly lucky I am to have my wonderful husband. I looked at his face, red eyes and pursed lips. I held his hand and told him he was so lucky to have such a lovable man for a father. We arrived a bit early and almost my whole family where there. I felt sad for Ben because there was only Georgia and Thomas from his. But my family is his too, they love Ben and they loved Peter and all Ben's friends where there for Peter too. He was such a big part of everyone's lives, special occasions, parties and holidays. We left the cars and entered the crematorium. Beautiful words were spoken. Ben did a eulogy that said I was his rock. "A ray of sunshine in the morning and his warm blanket at night". I cried. I wasn't the only one. We went to the coffin and we placed out hands upon it and I gave him a kiss goodbye before I left. The priest was wonderful. He made a leaflet for everyone with pictures of Peter and mentions of all of his hobbies. It was so personal and my emotions just exploded, I tried to be strong for Ben but I just completely let go. At the end of the service Conway Twitty came on and I laughed as the music plays although Peter and my sons love it. When we left we found a sunny spot for the flowers and went to the wake over the road. There were a lot of people and many stories where exchanged. Today was Peters day. But I was very proud of my husband and Georgia too.

Thursday.
Well what do you no Rose is contesting the will. She thinks! We received an email describing why she didn't visit her dad. One reason was because he treated her like crap as a child and the other was because she had a throat

infection, for three months. So which one is it? If she hated him that much why want his money? Erm... money grabber maybe? Anyway we've taken legal advice and the solicitor just laughed and said Peter had already prepared for this in his will as he expected it. Georgia also got an email accusing her that she'd already killed one parent, does she really want to kill another? I feel bad for Rose in a way; she obviously has a lot of issues. Maybe she should buy a few more cats! Ben went to see his mum and she just acted like nothing had happened, he went crazy. Ben doesn't do crazy. His mum just stuck up for Rose over and over and put down his father and told him he set it all up to take his money. I'm so glad we did everything right and legally. Bens mum started to cry but he told her any further contact can be threw a solicitor. Harsh but that woman has as many issues as her daughter.

Friday. Well what a surprise this morning Ben gets a text from Rose and then another email. She's either mentally ill or constantly drunk but that woman is making no sense. Don't disown your father for two years and then try and take my sons inheritance he left them. And don't slag off my husband when he's nursed your father through cancer and you were nowhere to be seen.

Saturday. And yet another email comes.

Ben replied "if you have anything else to say please go through our solicitor or this will be deemed as harassment". We just filed the nonsense of the troubled one and went to Lotherton Hall. It was a bright summer morning and the children were really excited. We spent lots of time in the bird garden and the old manor house. It was just such a relaxing slow and calm family day. The only thing missing was Peter in his hat and his wispy white moustache. That evening Ben and I made pasta and homemade meatballs. I had chicken and even made my own pesto. I suppose there's a sense of satisfaction about making your food from scratch.

Sunday. Pub tonight with my friend Anita. I

really should remember to invite Lulu along one night, I think they'll get on really well. That's the things with my friends, none of them know each other. It's a shame really because all my mates are really down to earth, no airs and graces and very grounded. Not a bitch among them.

Monday. At four am Ben left for a fishing trip he had been looking forward too since his birthday. On Ben's birthday the doctors told him his dad only had a few weeks so I think that will always stay with him. He went with all his friends and was really excited.

Tuesday. Things are getting really nasty and I'm feeling really bad for Georgia. She's done nothing wrong, neither of us has but from what I've been told Rose was really nasty to her regarding Georgia's daughter and she was in tears. Thomas came home from work which I think helped but we'll stick together and get through this. This situation just makes me laugh. I pity Rose I feel sorry for her but Georgia's suffering and that's not on. I think Georgia will end up moving away.

Wednesday. Rose has dropped her feeble attempt to contest the will. She's all bloody mouth! She dropped the drama because she was threatened with the contact of others in her life that actually does mean something to her.

Ben and I went for a walk and had lunch at our local pub. It was fun to spend time with him after his fishing trip and just to talk and kind of, get back on the same page. After all these years he still makes me laugh those really big deep belly laughs that make me trump. He just needs to sort his mother out now. The only problem with that is, he doesn't care if he ever sees her again and that's a big deal for Ben, he's generally so laid back he's laid down with a cup of cocoa.

Thursday.

Well we did the school run and Ben went to college. After a bit of painting I decided anything in the house had more importance than the painting. I was bored to death. So I went out. I went to our local farm for some dinner and got a new lamp for our bedroom. When Ben got home at lunchtime we had some news. There was a bit of a discrepancy with a small policy Peter had been paying into. It was thought that the will would override it but it works out Rose is entitled to a third. We have been told all along by Rose that if she received any money she would split the money between the three grandchildren. As apparently it's not about the money. I tell you now, if she is sent a cheque, she WILL keep it. But I don't really care if she spends the whole lot on a rubber dingy, cuddly toy or a pair of those sucks in pants.

Personally she needs to pay for some therapy and classes in common decency and manners.

The only elephant in the room is Ben's mum Hyacinth. It really feels like Ben couldn't care less if he never sees her again. Moses's birthday is coming up and regarding hyacinth I don't know how that will work. Ben and I have both agreed hyacinth will never look after Noah and Moses again. She's malicious and vicious and that's not the environment we want our sons to be in, especially if Rose turned up. Our children are extremely impressionable. But they do love their grandparents and as long as Ben is there when they go to visit then I am ok with that. She will be shown the emails Rose sent, not because Ben wants to cause trouble but Rose is obsessed with accusing her dad for her "bad childhood". The emails say very differently and are a complete attack on hyacinth.

Friday. So today was D day and it was time to kick that elephant out of the room. Ben and I spoke over and over about whether or not he should call her or get her husband out of the way and speak to her alone. In the end we realised to really get everything he needed to say he would have to send an email from the two of us. After all, the two of us are affected by this continually. Ben spoke to Georgia but she wasn't very happy as she believed it would stir up trouble between Rose and Georgia again. Rose could stir up trouble with her own reflection, its sheer boredom. We understand that because Georgia and Thomas live in Roses house and are kind of tenants that we don't want to do anything to jeopardise their situation. But Georgia has to understand that she has spoken too her mother and although we don't know what has been said the ice between them has been broken. Ben's problems will not end until he says his piece. Ben sat up until 3am re wording the email, we decided to leave out the nasty texts and emails as this would add fuel to the fire for Georgia and that's the last thing we wanted. In the morning I had a look over it and it was sent, it read as follows……………………..

Mum,

I have so much to say but I fear it will only fall on deaf ears, so I will keep it as short as possible. Emma and I don't want you to stop seeing the children because they love you but they will never be left alone with you again. If you love them just as much you will make more of an effort. We can't afford to allow them to be in any sort of unhealthy poisonous environment.

The last few months have been very straining on my family (including the kids) but as a very close family and with the support from all of Emma's family, and friends, we got through it. We had good times as well as the obvious sad ones, but I will never regret doing what we did for dad. You and Rose were NOT there, therefore you know nothing! It was never for monetary gain as you accused me of (maybe your judging me by your own standards, but I thought you knew your son better) I got nothing in the will.

The way Rose behaved before and after dad passed away was appalling. I will never forgive her and as far as I am concerned I have only one sister. I have my own loving respectful family that doesn't play silly games or play their kids off against each other. I have always known Emma has just tolerated you for my sake. We had excuse after excuse from Rose as to why she didn't turn up, yet it took his death for an excuse to be put forward. Funny how as soon as the will came out she became a lot more interested in the situation, contesting the will was no surprise but my dad was prepared for that in his will. So who's the real money grabber? It was not me, as you accused me of. But still, we kept her updated continually; we all did the right thing!

We received many texts and emails from Rose; these are not included because this matter needs to end. I am accused of murder and perhaps manipulation of my father's mind. Unfortunately for her, he was of sound mind (with full medical records to prove it 58 hrs before he died!) I am also told that I am going to kill you too! Amazing! Your daughter is so messed up, none of which is my fault as all the emails confirmed (you don't have to be a genius to work out whose fault it is...yours!). It's clear she's very troubled and needs some help. It's strange that in her emails there seems to be a constant pattern of her blaming you for her terrible childhood, with huge resentment towards me. Rose has issues and she has a right to them, but don't we all, Emma had the worst things possible happen to her as a child but some people blame the world for their issues and hang ups, others take the positives from the negatives and move on. This tragic event has shed light on team Rose and Hyacinth vs. the world. No one is perfect! I am still coming to terms with how messed up you both are, (I think you forget I've just lost my dad) I assure you I will not need therapy or be a "burden" to anyone, Emma and I will stand tall, heads high and move forward on our own.

I don't think you will change your ways...Rose never will. I walked away from you because you went straight to Rose as the emails proved. My family will come before everyone, even when we had to dress my dad sometimes, or clean him after accidents it was an honour for Emma and I, all the time though no monetary gain was thought about, as I have been accused of trying to get. I received nothing from my dad's estate, except bills which I am still taking care of! All Emma and I got was an immense sense of pride, joy and warmth from caring for a human being who had been told he had 2 months to live! I was told this on my birthday by my dad as he cried to me! I nagged all the time as you know, and it was me that had to tell him that she wasn't coming (because he asked now and then, he was ill not stupid), then watched as he fought back tears, he had just been told it had spread to his spine 4 hours previously. Kick a man when he's down. I could go on and on, maybe you will experience this one day and have an epiphany.

I'm a good man and believe you have treated me appallingly but one day you will be left all alone if you carry on like this. I have had spats with you before, and you change for a while and then go back to being your old self. You're just not a very nice person and that's the fact of it. Up until a few months ago I would have been there for you as I was dad (as would Emma). So it's up to you mum, change for the better, or live the rest of your life bitter and twisted. But we will have no involvement in that, my life is moving forward with or without you.

You always told us "when you can look in the mirror and see someone perfect staring back, you can have an opinion" you have one in the kitchen…

Ben and Emma.

This was mild; it's hard as a reader to not see past the pettiness. But these are real emotions that have built up over years and years and took a wonderful man's death to come to a head.

Saturday.
Ben said something interesting to my today. He believes his mother is jealous of me, I can see where he's coming from, I think she would have been happy having him on the tit on our honeymoon! If that's true maybe she should be grasping onto every olive branch, piece of love or wolf whistle from builders she can get, that's serious insecurity. No reply yet, but I am happy with a drama free day.

Sunday.
We went to Harewood House today. Moses was in a strange mood and I could tell something was on his mind. I asked if anything was wrong and he said he missed granddad. He asked where granddads body went and if he was in heaven. It's so hard to explain to a little boy who doesn't understand the world about death. I just want to hold on to him and love him so much that he's never sad again. It's funny; they haven't once mentioned Hyacinth and granddad. I suppose that's sad in itself.

Monday.
Today I will be mostly having gas.

Tuesday.
You know there's a time in your life when it can be quite simply put into three

sections. Weddings, christenings and funerals, the decisions we make and the actions we take determine the timing of the three life events. In my twenties I had a wedding a month to go too. They were the best events, happy tears, dancing, gala melon starter and a sorbet course if you were posh. There was so much positivity in the air. I'm smiling because I am talking as though I was ancient. The christenings, seriously? I think a lot of people nowadays just want a bit of a knees up or are just planning ahead for the pick of their favourite school. They are so unbelievably boring but I suppose you get to get dressed up and eat a load of "mums been to Iceland" crap afterwards. Then there are the funerals. So reflective and sad, but still sometimes have a glimmer of hope, that you will live a life to its fullest from now on. For some this can be the case but for others it's short lived. But for one thing, it shouldn't take the death of a loved one to realise life is too short to waste it.

Wednesday.

Jesus it was hot today. I feel like I have done a million and one things today but haven't actually achieved anything. Ben and I took Georgia and Thomas to Halifax so she could buy a car. It was in good shape but wow did it take a long time. My body is actually half burnt because I have driven so much. I was really pleased for her; she spent the money Peter left her for something really worthwhile. It's an automatic so Ben and I will be teaching her to drive. I can't wait to get started, she's determined and I know she'll do it.

Thursday.
I booked five days in Centre Parcs today. The family fund gave us a grant for £500. It kind of made me feel a bit positive and have something to look forward to. I got the booking as close to Moses's birthday as I could; unfortunately both kids have their birthdays in the holidays so any holidays cost a fortune. Moses, yet again was sent home for been sick. There was nothing wrong with him, although he claimed he had been sick and flushed it away. I just wish the school would wise up.

Friday.
My mum called me today. She told me that she has to go into hospital in eight days. She will be there for ten days and will be in a wheel chair for six weeks. She became quite and started to cry and put down the phone. It's got me down a bit but I told her we will all be there for her and whatever she needs we will sort it out for her. My mum just isn't one to except help. But with a

major back operation, she won't have much choice.

Saturday.
Peter left the boys some money. It's not a huge amount but certainly is a great addition to there already growing savings. It's a nice feeling to save for your children; I just wish I could save more.

Sunday.
I looked at Noah today and he looked so sad. I asked him in a quite manner what was wrong; he told me his friends won't play with him anymore because they say he's different to them. My heart just bled. I cuddled him but he pushed me away. I know the child he's talking about. Ignorant, spoilt, a fat headed product of his own ridiculous parents. I told him I will sort it and I will, I would love to speak to his mum but I know I have to go through the right channels. I promised Noah that in a couple of weeks, he and I would spend the day together, when I said a school day he smiled. Ok I know I shouldn't take him out of school for the day but we need time together, Noah and mum.

Monday.
I'm now certain we will have no reply from Hyacinth and I am kind of happy with

that although I am sad for the children. She obviously doesn't care enough for them to want to sort things out. Well I suppose she's lost out, she isn't too bright so she'll never realise how much. I woke up feeling so sick this morning but I managed to get to school with Ben and speak to Noah's teacher about the boy bullying him. She said she would have a word. I don't actually think she took it seriously but if it gets worse ill push the issue as far as I can until it is sorted. And it will get sorted.

Tuesday.

Its, breakfast, lunch and dinner! I hate it when people call dinner tea. It's not a northern thing and it's not a trying to be posh thing, it's just a right thing!. Well that's what Wikipedia says……………………………so it must be true!

Wednesday.

Ben had the day off today so I wanted to make as much of the day about us spending time together. But, that didn't happen. I already knew we had invited Moses's friend poppy for dinner so was going to prepare a nice meal for them of homemade burgers and chips with a nice desert to finish it off. Ben and I spent most of the day at B&Q, Screwfix and my grandmothers fitting lights for her and new plug sockets. My mums made my grandma's house her little project so she's been busying herself painting and putting new banister rails up. It looks great but I can't help thinking she's trying to do as much independent jobs as she can before she's completely immobile. I suppose I can't blame her for that.

Thursday.
Early this morning I took Moses to the dentist. I bloody hate his dentist. Pompous, looks about fifteen, arrogant and speaks down to people. He gets on my bloody nipple ends. Every time I go in there he says the same thing. "Give him less pop and sweets and make sure he brushes everyday". Don't assume I have no education, don't assume I'm a bloody idiot and don't assume I won't key your "substitute for a tiny cock convertible"............................ (For legal reasons, I am obviously joking). The tooth that has a tiny hole in is a milk tooth so that made me feel a lot better. I actually can't type about him anymore because he's a twat.

Friday.
I took Georgia for a driving lesson today and I was really impressed. We drove all the way from south Leeds to Fitzwilliam to Thomas's mum's house to drop a few bits off for Flora's stay. They were lovely down to earth

people that were the kind of people who put you at ease straight away. I love people who have no heirs and graces; I call them, a spades a spade type. Pretty much like my whole family, especially my grandma. Driving to Fitzwilliam was quite relaxing with only a few minor hiccups. On the way back and probably because we didn't stop talking she made a few mistakes. We approached a roundabout and Georgia pulled out onto a car. I had to laugh at my own reaction. I didn't shout I just started jumping around and clicking my fingers in the direction I wanted her to go in, which she didn't go in. We got home safe and she even did a great parallel park. After I got back in my car I couldn't stop laughing. It's nice to have a giggle, kind of like a free anti-depressant substitute. I was expecting a big romantic meal when I got home as I asked Ben to go and buy something nice for dinner. I got mackerel some pesto and a weight watchers yogurt. Yep, romance is dead.

Saturday.
Noah was a bit sad last night. He has it in his head that I'm going to leave him and never return. It takes just the slightest of things, such as a cartoon, overhearing a conversation or a dream he had. I decided it was a good idea to spend some time with just him. We

went up to my grandmas as he likes it there. I think it's the reclining sofa, juice and as many custard creams she can ram down his neck that he likes. After grandma's house, I took him to Tesco's to get a few "jubilee" weekend dinner treats, and it was Noah's turn to choose desert. Noah was smiling most of the couple of hours we spent together and that made me happy. When we got home Ben and Moses had come back from Ikea with a yucca plant called Geoff.

Sunday.

Today feels like it's been a bit wasted. It's the queen's jubilee so I have been watching the 1000 ships going down the Thames. I love been British, for all the little things, like still been determined to have fun outside even in the rain. Moses has been quite testing; he seems to need more and more attention, which means I give Ben and Noah less. I sometimes have great guilt but I have to continue to try and even out my time with everyone.

Mondays. Lily told me she's getting married, which is fantastic. She said she's going to Malta and would I go. I told her I would if she wanted me too, I think she just wanted a yes id love too but it was obvious by my face I didn't want to go to Malta. I hate abroad and the heat. Lily and I aren't as close as we were and I hope that changes soon because I love her to bits. She was my role model growing up. If Lily is truly happy, then I am really happy for her. She's had a lot of loneliness and I hated seeing her so sad. Woo hoo I get to wear a nice dress.

Tuesday.

Today I went to Clarins with my friend Laura. I love Laura to bits. We had a great joint massage and had a look around the shops. I told her not to get the aromatherapy massage. You come out looking like you've been in a chip pan! We had lunch at Nandos (living it large) mind you any time spent with my friends is always time well spent. Mums in hospital tomorrow, I hope she does well. Love you mum.

Wednesday.

My mum went into hospital today. She went really early on so I have been calling all day. The hospital is horrendous and just speaks to people like crap. I finally got hold of her but it was way too late to visit. She sounded quite perky, which is great considering she's just had a back operation. I'm looking forward to seeing her tomorrow and I'll be taking her lots of diet coke.

Thursday.

I, my grandma, my dad and Noah went to see my mum today. I went up to the ward and she was waiting for me with a kind of," I am really trying to look happy face on". I took her down to Costa where everyone was waiting. Mum was on morphine and was talking total shite, slightly embarrassing. Noah was happy though as everyone kept on feeding him. So my mum had three cigs and we had a little chat. She thinks she's getting out by a week on Friday. She's dreaming!

Friday.

You know when something is really upsetting you but you can't shake the feeling off. It makes you feel sick inside. I have felt like this for the most of today until I spoke to Ben. And then felt worse. Last night Noah was crying and asking why he doesn't see Nan anymore. It was almost as though he was blaming me for it. I felt sick and really didn't know what to tell him. All day I have wanted to send her a text and tell her to either buck her ideas up where her grandchildren are concerned or at least tell us she isn't interested so I can make up some elaborated story and keep on buying them gifts from her. I never want them to know that she doesn't care. But one day they will know the truth because there is no way I will get the blame for her cold, sick actions. I can't honestly say I won't confront her. If I have a problem, it gets sorted out. I hate that sick nervous feeling.

As we thought Rose has received her cheque and she obviously won't be giving it to her niece and nephews. Money grabbing, uneducated, vile piece of shit. God I wish I could shout that from the rooftops.

Saturday.

I've gone mad. Last night I wrote an email to Ben's mum but I didn't send it. When you can hear the whimpers and the emotion coming from your child's bedroom, because he can't see his Nan, it's heart-breaking. I just lost it, as Ben watched on I typed furiously until I had beads of sweat running down my face. But all the time I just wanted to go round and speak to her myself. She's not the kind of woman you could have an intelligent conversation with, if you know what I mean. I actually like her husband. I mean he's the most hen pecked man I have ever met but you can have a sensible conversation with him. I kind of see him as the IRA and her as Al-Queada. You can sit and have a chat with one but the others, just plain deluded, anyway enough wasting time on my Jeremy Kyle style scenario.

Myself, Ben and the kids took my mums new wheelchair we got for her today. She liked it and as her other hasn't turned up she has no option. She hopped about and I chatted with her for a while. I was a bit pissed with her yesterday and I told her if Moses gets a card from Rose we will be sending it back, in person. I really understand that this seems very petty as it's not Moses's fault. But, Rose will have no input or involvement in my children's life anymore, although her husband is more than welcome. The emails we received accusing us of killing her dad was the last straw. Ben only has one sister now, only really ever did to be honest………………………………………………………………
……………..

I've just got really sad and called Georgia. I think she's the only one that has some insight into the way I feel regarding the kids relationship with their Nan. I drove over in my pyjamas (very Kerry Katona) and we sat in her kitchen and had a good chat that made me feel a lot better. Georgia suggested that Ben asks his mum to go on a dog walk with her and the kids. When I got home I told Ben and after a long chat and a rather stressful hour he agreed to ask his mum to meet up. Maybe they'll have a chat, maybe Barney will kick off or maybe just maybe they'll sort things out for the sake of the kids and it will be a productive afternoon. God knows we need one of them!.

Sunday.
Its father's day. Plus our anniversary dinner with all the family, I can feel it; today's going to be a good day.

The dinner was great and not as expensive as I thought. I planned for a couple of hundred pound but it came to just less than that, which is good as no one wanted desert so I saved there.

We seem to live in an even more of a class system nowadays. It's moved down a notch. It doesn't seem to be so looked down upon to be struggling. In a way this is good, I think I'd like a classless society, but this is England so it's not going to happen. Today really was a good day.

Monday.
Ben has sent his mum a text asking if she will meet him close to where she lives with the kids for a dog walk. We thought it would be best for Ben and his mum to meet somewhere neutral. She text back, four hours later and agreed for tomorrow. As long as it

wasn't raining! We'll see. Cod and chips for dinner? Don't mind if I do.

Tuesday.

I'm getting that very anxious and feel constantly sick regarding Ben's mother. I just want things to go well for my little boys. Am I just clinging to the fact that I am desperate for a hugely unemotional woman to want to see and love her grandchildren? Bloody hell I think I'm the deluded one.

Well that's it. Ben met up with his mum and it wasn't positive at all. Moses didn't even want to go but they went for a walk and Barney was up Ben's mums arse the whole time, no emotion was exchanged either. At one point Ben got a second with his mum and said "so where do we go from here"? She replied "well I am not going to stop talking to Rose if that's what you think". Ben at this moment realised he was flogging a dead horse and that she obviously didn't understand what he was getting at and took the kids home. When Ben got home he explained all this to me and kneeled down and just said "I think it's time we cut all ties, including the kids". I finally agreed, reluctantly because I really want my sons to know their grandparents. I still to this day wish she would wake up and realise what she's lost. I want my kids to have a Nan and granddad but sometimes even members of your family have to be let go. This is the email we sent, I think Ben's emotions where running quite high when he wrote it but the facts are there, and his true feelings.

Mum,

Emma and I have unfortunately had to contemplate your involvement with our sons many times before, but have always believed it was in our children's interest to know you and their grandfather. It's become blatant it isn't as important to you. Going on your parenting skills and non-existent efforts to attempt to acknowledge them, it's clear you don't provide a stable environment for them and you in particular are not the kind of role model I want around my very impressionable children. We have no option but to cut all ties with you both. I do not wish to be a burden to you.

Your family values are draconian and quite frankly sickening. You've lost your only son and now your grandchildren. You just won't see sense and that's very sad, for you. But it only brings us a great sense of relief.

It's obvious you hold great favouritism and are content with being Rose's puppet. You're scared to speak to me, one to one without Barney or "others" up your backside, like any loving mother would. But of course Barney always comes first (as he has done in the past), yet so does my wife and family too, your loss! I hope Rose enjoys her money that was left to Noah and Moses!

My children have four grandmothers, three grandfathers, 18 cousins, 3 uncles, 7 great uncles, 3 aunties, 6 great aunties and the best mum and dad in the world. My family will more than compensate for your loss. You're clearly clutching at straws and I have great pity for your loneliness it must be terrible only having a few people who care for you. It's almost as if you have been brainwashed by Rose, I never asked you to choose!

So we want no more contact, that includes Barney which is unfortunate as I have nothing against him (who my son loves playing chess with) our children will be sheltered from these events, but one day they will know. The sad thing is you really don't know what you've lost!. Let's hope you never meet them in the street, how would you react then?

Ben and Mrs Emma Plows BSc Hons.   <----
---oh look, real letters after Emma's name, mine are to follow...

Ben's mum once did a NVQ so used to tell us she had letters after her name! Something she relished.

Wednesday.
Today I have been expecting Barney to come and bang on my door. All I would do is quite calmly asked him to come in and have a cup of tea and we can have a chat. Sometimes he can be rational; you just have to get him away from his wife.

Thursday.
Sometimes I wish I could say every little detail that is in my mind. But I can't. I'd be sued of beaten up. It doesn't make sense and people wouldn't like it and why would I want to make people sad. If only the world was as simple as been able to be exactly who you wanted to be and behave in a way that suited you.

Friday. Well what a boring day. Facebook status: just because I don't polish, clean, vac, wash and iron everything in sight every single day doesn't mean I am lazy. It means life's too short and I have better things to do. Like………………………………………………………
………………stuff!

If I had a pound for every time someone said,

Mam, mam can I have some jam and bread.

Of course I am only cleaning and cooking,

But pull out my third arm and I am sure I can do anything.

And also, could I please have a cuddle and sweets and feed the snake,

Sure, sure and if you want ill even bake you a cake.

Give me a second, a moment some peace,

But for fucks sake get me off of this flaming leash.

Saturday.
I've been practicing making cupcakes furiously today. I have to get them just right. But I have realised that you can cover anything up with icing. I'm giving Georgia a driving test tonight; I might talk her into just going for a coffee.

Sunday. This diary was supposed to be a form of self-help but it seems to be a reminder of my constant moaning at the minute. I suppose these are just my private thoughts though and if I can't be honest with my diary, when can I be?

Monday. I've been feeling increasingly more down lately. So today my routine; visit to my psychiatrist came just in time. As soon as I sat down in the waiting room I noticed I had three missed calls from Lily, one from my mum and two from Ben. As you can imagine signs like this only mean something bad has happened. I immediately ran outside, and rang Lily. She told me my mum had been taken into the hospital. They didn't know if it was her appendicitis or MRSA. Her stomach was really painful after her operation. I had to go to Noah and Moses's sports day and I began to feel really guilty. I had a long conversation with Dr Wong about how bad I felt that I couldn't decide whether I should go to my mum or the kids. I seemed to be stuck in this mental crying, sobbing over dramatic rut. After I had spoken to him for a while regarding other things in my life he handed me a form and I filled in all the questions. He devised from this that I had depression. No shit Sherlock, Miss Marple has nothing on you! I can't believe he had to do that and couldn't see this himself. Maybe this is how it's supposed to be diagnosed. I'm no stranger to depression but I thought that was in my past. I was just getting used to been levelled out or slightly manic. Depression can be a killer but I feel in no way suicidal, I'm just feeling really sad. Anyway, my lithium has been put up as antidepressants make me high. Let's hope I feel better soon. I eventually went to the sports day only to be faced with Noah rocking and crying on the field. He was been completely ignored by his assistant. I just snapped. I walked down onto the field and got him. I informed the assistant that after six years it was blindly obvious that sports day distresses Noah and he won't be doing it again. I'm not putting my son through this anymore. I understand Noah has to join in but the curriculum has to adapt to Noah, not the other way round. Because THAT'S THE LAW!!!!

My mum had to sit in the hospital A & E for hours. They sent her home and have told her to come back tomorrow after ruling out any imminent concerns; although a CT scan is needed and she seems ok.

Tuesday.

I went to visit my mum today. Ben had taken her to the hospital at 8:30 this morning to yet again wait for help. Has my mum really been waiting in A&E for two days? When I arrived she seemed in high spirits but was still waiting, be it on a holding ward. I gave her the clothes she needed and we went outside so she could smoke. Ben and the kids were waiting for me in the car so I went and told her I was there if she needed me. Yet again she said she'd be fine when it was obvious she was worried. All I do is say I am there; it's up to her if she takes the help.

Wednesday.

All night I have been throwing up and evacuating on the crapper. I am so ill both ends are burning and I just want to sleep. I haven't called my mum but Ben did nothing to tell really. Shit day.

In my head I am begging, begging for love and your embrace,

When I need your help and care, the rejections written all over your face.

If you had just wanted me and hadn't pushed me away,

Maybe, just maybe I wouldn't have turned out this way.

Don't get me wrong I can't blame bipolar on you,

But your lack of affection has been damaging and that's true.

Thursday. I love Ben. I'm so lucky to have a partner for life that gives me minimal grief and is a great dad. He doesn't try to tell me how to think or bosses me about. I'm my own woman but yet still securely sheltered by a wonderful caring man. I was out for a run with my friend and on a beautiful night I was reminded of how lucky I and my family are. I'm not rich; I can pay my bills and go to Centre Parcs twice a year.

Friday. For Fucking, shagging, pissing, wanking, frigging (is frigging female masturbation?) shitting, twatting scrotums sake! This morning I got a call from Lily asking me why I hadn't gone to see my mum in hospital this week. I've actually been twice but because I missed two days as I have been throwing up and looking for a cork to stick up my arse I didn't go. Not because I didn't want too, but because I was infectious and I am certainly not going into a hospital so I can pass it on to very sick people. Lily disagreed and informed me she's sick of hospitals and I should make more effort. At that point I had had enough and put down the phone. I don't actually believe Lily knows how hurtful she can be. I go to my mums at least three times a week; I ring four times a week, at least. I take her everywhere and offer my help but to her and apparently my mum this isn't good enough. I don't know who the bitch is; my mum for lying to lily about my lack of visits or Lily for believing her and gobbing off. Should I really be surprised? I've felt really sad all day. But I can't change them and everyone I have spoken to has asked me why I am so surprised, in all honesty I'm not, but it still hurts. Anyway my mums had her operation and she rang me at three to say she's coming home. So we picked her up and while Ben took her home I had me CT scan. Tomorrows a new day, and apparently I am making Noah and Moses breakfast in bed!

Saturday.

I've laughed a lot today. It's wonderful to have those real family days and have genuinely enjoyed them. Instead of doing those kids activities because you feel you have too. Ben made the kids pancakes in bed and

Millie came round quite early on with my gorgeous nephew.

Sunday.
Good god I am unfit. Today was great. I did the race for life, for Peter. I really do feel like my day has had some purpose today. Myself, Georgia, Millie and her friend Kelly ended up in the walking group. I have never wanted to run as much in my life. There must have been thousands of women at the race for life and the atmosphere was wonderful. You know when I was lining up waiting to start the race I saw so many peoples pictures and messages on their backs stating why they were doing the race, it was quite emotional. I really felt like I was doing something special. It was lovely to talk to Georgia on the way round; I don't think we have ever chatted for so long. It took a total of ninety minutes to walk five kilometres, why? Well I am not that unfit but it's amazing the problems and hold ups puddles and mud can cause. My mum came with us all and I think she enjoyed herself; it was nice to have the support. Today was a really good day.

Monday.
I don't care what the look is; men with an ample arse and a muscly body should never wear skinny jeans and a tight vest. Well,

unless you're gay! I've felt quite good today, health wise.

Thursday.
When Ben came home today from doing his Warhammer club I could tell by the look on his face that Moses had done something wrong. Ben told me that Moses had "head-butted" his teaching assistant. I was horrified, Moses is always getting into trouble but this just made me feel sick.

Friday.
Last night I found a piece of paper with a picture of his teaching assistant on it, it was ripped up and it was under his pillow. When I asked him why he had done it he just stared at me and started to cry, he held his breath and started to shake. Eventually he told me that his teaching assistant had been poking him in the chest. Moses can sometimes tell lies but I have never ever been more certain that my son was telling the truth. Or what he believed was the truth.

I called the school and told them I was not going to bring Moses in because he was too upset and I wanted to find out what had happened before I sent him back. I went up and spoke to someone, I wasn't happy but in the end it was decided that she would no longer work with Moses.

Monday.

Well today's the day and where all excited where off to Centre Parcs. The weather is bloody awful but this is England and rain or shine we will have fun!

After our ninety minute drive to Nottingham I was absolutely starving, we dumped our bags in the log cabin and trotted off to the park burger restaurant. I have a feeling my family healthy eating is going to go right out of the window. Burgers, chips, curry, deserts and hot chocolate never hurt anyone, Right? I'm on holiday, I'm certainly not doing the "perfect mum" thing.

Tuesday.

So that's six activities booked and I am officially skint two days into our holiday. But I don't mind, the weather has had a real change around and the air smells sweet. I'm in a really positive mood today and the kids are all smiles. I have had a run in with a couple of swans that I thought were sleeping, but really weren't. Jesus those things are just plain vicious. Don't they all belong to the queen? She can have the crazy buggers back!

Wednesday.

I made a point of going for a quick walk by myself today. I walked in the sunshine wearing my new low cut pink short playsuit. I felt quite attractive, I've lost two stone since Peter died and have finally achieved my pre pregnancy weight. It only took me ten years! I got myself a hot chocolate and met up with Ben and the kids in the sub-tropical pool. I didn't go into the pool but I did sit on a sun lounger next to it in my new cut away swimsuit. Married men with their kids sometimes are really quite pervy, Cheeky buggers.

Thursday.

Moses, Noah and I all went for a ride in a horse and carriage. We've been on this one before and Moses even remembered the horse was called Gandalf. I always get really nervous when my children come into contact with new people because I never know how they will behave and what they will say. I'm not embarrassed of my children, to me they are perfect but people just don't understand them and they look at my sons as if they are stupid. This upsets me and can really piss me off. You're never more protective over your children than when an adult becomes annoyed at something they've done and just won't take your explanation, I just want to shake some intelligence into them.

Thursday.
Ben is going to the spa tonight and I'm going to have my traditional massage and facial. Oh I love to be pampered. When Ben goes this evening I'll let the kids stay up late so we can watch a DVD and make our dinner on the barbecue. The kids have always gone to bed at half seven and we have had this routine since they were two months old. Now they are getting older I have told them they can stay up until eight but because they have such a strong routine they still insist on getting their pyjamas on at seven and supper at seven fifteen. The worst time is in the winter when Noah notices the moon coming out at four o'clock and tries to get ready for bed. Bless my perfect, innocent little boys.

Friday.
Well today we go home and none of us wants to go. If I had enough money we would defiantly stay longer. I'm going to let the kids go to the big sweet shop for on the way home, just to keep them quiet but this weekend is going to have to be a crap food free weekend otherwise that idiot dentist really will have a reason to look down on me. Ha what is it with the middle classes?

Saturday

I haven't been out properly into Leeds since my birthday. Tonight I'm going out with four of my friends to Greek street and maybe brewery's wharf.

I'm shitfaced, but not only am I pissed I am sat on the toilet and think I will be for some time. I wish alcohol didn't make me force every fluid in my body to escape. Even my nose is running. Well that's it I certainly won't need another bum goblin for a while. I'm smiling, because I just love toilet humour, or arse filth. No not arse filth. I'm still smiling. I'm giggling now.

Sunday.

I got up at eleven this morning and Ben has no sympathy for me. I usually go for a really long jog on a Sunday but today there was no chance. I'm glad I went out last night and had a dance; it was a lot of fun. I'm starting to realise at the grand old age of thirty four I am getting way too old for short dresses above the knee. Don't get me wrong I think I look great and all my mates say I did and I certainly get a lot of looks, but I'm starting to feel conscious. I can still look good and dress nice but I think it's time to get a new going out wardrobe.

Noah and I did his preparations for his last transition visit before he starts high school. It all builds up to this. I do like the school and we have had many meetings regarding my concerns but I can't help but worry. I just want them to understand my son so he has a great school life that he can be happy with. He has funding for one to one support and a great statement that I recently had amended; he's met his teacher, senco, assistant and head of year. I'm as happy as I can be at this point.

Little boy you're growing into a man so fast,

As soon as I blink the day away I am already looking back into the past.

Your maturity had begun to astound me,

I feel so rich that all this love is at this moment just for me.

From a baby to my little clever clone,

You bring the feelings out in me of which I am not prone.

Please grow to be a great man just like your dad,

I'd feel the luckiest mum my Moses, with you I'll never be sad.

Monday.

After a cuppa at my favourite neighbour Lulu's house I went up to Tesco's (do I actually write this crap down?) I was just about to go pay for my gammon and eggs and this man came up to me and started to stare at me. I felt really uncomfortable, he handed me a card with his number on and then shuffled off really quickly. I started to giggle, how childish I am. I soon stopped giggling when I saw him walk away with a pushchair, vile!

Tuesday.

Only four days left until the school holidays and Ben is at home today, he's finally finished his college course and passed with flying colours. He only has to wait for his maths gcse result. I'm so proud of him, maybe I should tell him more often. So we went up to Calverly on the other side of Leeds and had the set menu for ten pound. It was actually very nice. Probably more calories in the chicken salad than my profiteroles but so what, I'm not dieting. But I should be exercising.

Wednesday.

I went up to see my mum today and she mentioned that her and my dad was going to Tenerife with my grandparents and did I want to go with her. She's also asking my brother and his wife. I'm not keen as I think it will be a lot of hard work and I'm worried about the kid's reaction to such a long flight. I will however feel a lot better if Joseph and Millie come and it will be great to have four out of the five generations all on holiday together. I think. So I'll talk to Ben and see if he shares my enthusiasm.

Thursday. Crap day nothing to report.

Oh, Ben gave Georgia a driving lesson today and she's been told she can take her test in two weeks. I'm really pleased for her and I'm sure shell pass. I sometimes wish me and her were closer; she said we could have Flora next week for the day so that will be nice.

Friday. Is Moses too young to be thrown out? That's how well today is going for Ben and I today. Moses is continually talking like a baby. He gets into these little phases where he has his funny ways, eating his clothes (pica), repeating naughty words and now its talking like a baby. The pitch of baby screams is too much; I'm becoming more and more frustrated. If I could scream that loudly at him that he was scared to death and thought twice about doing it again then

I would consider it, but he just doesn't get it. If I say stop he says "ok" in a baby's voice.

I can't be the only fucked up parent on this Earth,

Did I know from day one I was useless? Right from his birth

I'm pathetic aren't I; I can't even raise a child right,

I try so very hard but someone has stolen my bloody fight.

I had it earlier but someone must have needed it,

Because now I crying and moaning

Oh shit!

Saturday. Spent up. I've hurt my back and I have a painful stomach so I've spent most of the day ironing and shopping for holiday clothes online. EBay was a great invention, I don't mind spending a few pounds on second hand t-shirts and kaftans. I think it's quite sensible to do that when you have two kids growing like bean shoots. Noah has size ten feet now and he's only eleven years old.

Sunday. One of my problems is that I don't actually realise that the mean things I say to people sometimes could actually hurt their feelings. It's almost as though I don't believe I have the power to make anyone cry or to affect them emotionally. Am I emotionally mute to other people's emotions? If I think of the way I have behaved towards others and the things I have said with my quick sharp tongue in the past then I have been quite mean to some that really haven't deserved it. Strangers, friends and family members (excluding dumb and dumber) have all been on the receiving end of my crap. When I'm in the moment I just don't see how hurtful I can be. Is there a tablet for that?

Monday. I can't be arsed talking to an imaginary person today as I am far too important to discuss with you the ins and outs of my day. I have also decided that you are way too nosey and need to get yourself some friends and stop bugging me.

Dear Diary, I've only gone and booked Tenerife.

Tuesday. Made an origami wombat.

Wednesday. I picked up Moses and myself prescription today. Apparently when we go abroad next year I have to have a letter from my doctor for my Lithium and Moses Equasym and there controlled drugs and have a street value. Great, more expense.

Thursday. I have finally got round to cleaning underneath the two sofas today. That's the thing with wooden floors; you can see the dust building up in the corners of the room. Now we have a dog there's also a layer of our malting canines fluff building up too. I sit on the sofa watching television with an uneasy feeling down my back. I just know the hair and dust and probably a few of Moses apple cores down there too. So today I pulled them out, set myself a target of twenty minutes, turned MTV on and cleaned my arse off. Ah that's better.

Friday.

I'm going to have to tape my fat gob shut, not only do I seem to be offending everyone in sight but I'm slipping from a size twelve to a fourteen rather quickly. I just can't stop eating crap, plus I'm becoming a little more sociable lately and I'm having way too many meals out. I've decided to practice what I preach and go on a simple diet, it's only fair as I've told Noah he has to cut down on a lot of things. Considering I can't even get him to wear deodorant I don't quite know if he will be able to keep this in mind when it comes to school dinners.

Saturday.

I haven't got out of bed today. I woke up crying and this is always a sign that I'm getting a little down. I don't actually know why because life is good at the moment and it's easier to solve an issue that's upsetting you when you know why you're upset. Jon took the kids to a new park near us and I felt really guilty lying in bed when they were out. That's my problem I have far too much guilt when it comes to been a mother. Anyway I'm no good to the kids if I'm upset all the time so I'm going to stay where I am and hopefully I'll feel better tomorrow.

Sunday.

I said on Friday that I'm always offending people, well today it came to a head. There is a woman who lives near me and is one of the mums at the local school. I've seen her nearly every school day since 2004 but she's a little stand offish. Combined with me not liking to make new friends we were never likely to chat. I never had a problem with her until recently when she just started to blatantly stare at me. When someone stares at me for no reason I generally just stared back and give a bit toothy smile, and that's what I did today when I was walking the dog. Her reaction wasn't good and she just tutted and gave me a filthy look. I couldn't help it and I started to laugh so she just turned around on her heel and started to do her crazy staring trick again. I asked her what her problem was, apart from her hideously deformed face. She didn't like this and informed me that her friend had told her that her neighbour told her that I had called her a slag. Can you believe this crap? Am I back at St Michaels High? Throwing dirty looks and bitching? No, I'm Emma, mum of two and wife of student teacher. I told her if she had a problem that she only had to speak to me in a civil manner and I'm sure we could sort this out, but the fact that she would judge me and behave toward me so rudely really was a worse reflection on her than me. Her manner cooled and her facial expressions softened. The conversation went on for five minutes and it all pans out that apparently I did call her a slag, in 1992. She was from Middleton, the town I was raised in and as she remembers it was "darn t park in Miggy woods" how lovely. I know I was rude to her but I'm still laughing. I don't like arguing but I certainly won't shy away from it if I know I'm right. Some people huh?

Monday. Do you know, life is so much easier and stress free now Ben's mum isn't looming over us. I still think the situation is really sad though.

Tuesday. I pushed us all to go to Malham for a long walk today. Malham is a lovely place full of streams, forestry, campsites, hills and country pubs. It was a nice hot day and with a picnic and blanket we trotted off to the top of Malham hill (where the last harry potter was filmed) and ate our lunch on the hill watching the green fields and rolling hills. Then back down the hill to the pub for a glass of vino and some pork scratching's. How English.

Wednesday.

My medication is making me really forgetful and docile. Still I'm really lucky because I don't have to take anti-psychotics anymore and their real killers. Lithium just evens your mood out so I never get very high or very low. I still get irregular moods that are way out of the norm but I can recognise them. It's my new found space cadet dumbness that's the problem.

Thursday.

Georgia and Flora came up today for a cup of tea. It took me a whole twenty minutes to ask her how she got up here, to which she informed me she had passed her test the day before and had celebrated by driving the whole way to Scarborough last night to have fish and chips by the sea. I'm so happy for her, she used the money her father left her for something really useful and passed her test first time. Bloody star!

Friday.

In the same week I have joined the gym, I have also bought the hairy bikers book on pies. Well I figure if I'm going to be sweating in a council run gym with dozens of bored mothers, I can afford to eat the odd quiche Lorraine and cottage pie. Kind of when you have the mentality of "half the calories, you can eat twice as much" It works for me!

Saturday.

I'm having a friend crisis. I used to be really good friends with a girl called Larissa but she got a little needy on me. We didn't talk for a couple of years because she started to make me feel uncomfortable and I just blew her off and told her I was busy all the time. She started to get a little too interested in my life, especially my other friends and my kids. If I told her I was going out for lunch or to the pub with another friend shed want to know where and why I didn't invite her. I like friends who I don't have to explain myself too and I don't have pressure from to be there by their side every minute of the day. The thing was she didn't have much in her life other than lots and lots of men, and I'm happily married. Larissa was funny and had great dry wit which I think is the reason we originally hit it off but I started to get very nervous around her and I started to feel scared that she may scream something mean at me, again. I got abusive texts along the lines of "you're a fucking user, you'll never find a friend like me" you can say that again. I would also get comments like "dump the kids on Ben, your way too attached to them" "you wear far too much make-up" and "I'm going to kill myself" do it then you needy, abusive, insensitive moron!. In the end I had to change my number.

So, I have started to get friend requests on Facebook from her and I have ignored all four. Now to me I would have taken the hint but you have to have some issues if you know someone doesn't want to talk to you but you just keep pushing it. Bloody hell it's like single white female. Let's see how this one pans out, why do I attract the crazy's? Is it because they think I'm crazy? TAKE YOUR MEDS, JUST LIKE I DO!

Sunday. I got a phone call from my auntie this morning asking if Ben, myself and the kids want to go to her house and all the family were going for lunch for my grandmothers 93rd birthday. I love anything like this and cherish the times we all get together.

Is there anyone there to help her shut her fat gob,

Eating cheese, scoffing ham and picking at chocolate is making her fat tits blob,

I've heard that Mrs Plows will power has left the gym,

She's hiding in the cake shop filling up to the brim.

She says she's a size twelve but she's actually a fourteen,

Believe me stuffing that into a two piece should never be seen.

It will all be fine, she could starve for a week,

She will be thin she will be gassy; Mrs Plows really is the most beautiful freak.

Monday. Well it's the last day of the holidays for Noah and the first day back for Moses. I just couldn't get through to Moses that Noah's high school started a day later than his, but eventually he begrudgingly left the house with Ben and made there one minute journey in the car. Noah just stood there with a huge smile on his face, jumping up and down screaming "yeah, family fun day".

Tuesday.

I took Noah in this morning and I was very aware that I had to be continually upbeat and positive. I didn't leave many pauses of silence in the car and told him how great the day was going to be. He looked so smart and grown up in his uniform and I'm sure I saw a glint of pride through his disgruntled frown. I handed my precious little man over to a lovely teaching assistant and said my goodbyes. As soon as I got outside the tears started to flow and I just couldn't hold it together. The last seven years since his diagnosis have led up to this day. Jon and I went out for lunch at a nice country pub we know and had a long overdue natter, which ended up been all about the kids.

When the time came to get Noah he was waiting in reception for me with his assistant, he was really excited and started to tell me all about the games he had played and the pizza he had for lunch. I was told his day was great and he had done really well. I breathed a sigh of relief. I promised Noah and Moses I would take them to Pizza Hut after school to celebrate a fantastic start to their school week.

Wednesday.
I think getting into a routine once Ben starts university will be easier than I thought; it's just about managing my time properly. I have only ten minutes to get to Moses school near our house when I pick up Noah so I'll have to hurry up the chit chat with his teaching assistant at the end of the school day. But that's fine; I'm a bit unsociable anyway.

Thursday.
Today I met my friend in town and we went on our bi monthly shopping trip and ate crap at Nandos. I realised recently that it's me who has to make more effort when it comes to friends. So we had fun, chatted about our University days and the people we liked and disliked and spent way too much in a bunch of girly shops. After six weeks of kids, transformers, screaming kids and trips out it's nice to feel like Emma again.

Friday.
It's the end of the first week and I'm feeling positive about Noah's school and the way he feels about it. I can see PE is going to be an issue and he has to take ear defenders to his music lesson but apart from that it's going very well. Moses and I had a long chat tonight about where granddad spider went when he passed

away. Its so heart wrenching telling a little boy that his granddad is in a better place. I don't know the answers all I want to do is help my son through it and put his mind at rest but I'll never be able to fully achieve that. It's hard to explain death to an autistic child as they see things in a very black and white way, so it's difficult for them to understand anything different than he's in the ground. Moses kept asking when he was going to die and when I would die. I just want to climb in to that little boys head and fix his worries, because that's my job.

Over the last few months I have bonded with Moses more than the last few years. Where just so close now.

Saturday.
I've booked a colonic. I've had one before and they work wonders. I'm sick to death of been constipated and bloated. I continually look up the duff and it's starting to get painful so there's nothing else for it. There going in!

Sunday.
If my son's homework is only printing of pictures of the environment, is it really cheating to do it for him? When he was a primary school he got homework once a week and the

hysterics and physical violence against himself and others was terrible. If you imagine now he gets at least six pieces a week and although I am very aware that Noah has to do this on his own sometimes you just have to weigh your family life up. Is it really that important when I know he could end up biting himself or rocking until he has a complete meltdown? This isn't a naughty child having a tantrum. It's a distressed child having a breakdown. Granted it's not always that bad but we do get it at least once a week. We just have to pick our moments.

Emma's back

Monday. Just a look. That's all it took to scare the hell out of the kid who started to mimic Noah when he came out of school and excitably told me that he had had the best day ever. I am unbelievably protective over my sons and I think I have a huge chip on my shoulder when it comes to their diagnosis. It worries me that if when Noah gets older, if someone ever hurt him I would end up in prison. I just wouldn't be able to stay calm and be rational. He's so impressionable and trusting.

Tuesday.
It's nearly October which means it's time to get a real move on with the Christmas shopping. Oh yes it's that time of year again, excitement, drama, stress crying, and that's just me. I find Christmas very hard to deal with as it's so out of my routine. Noah's birthday is a few days before Christmas and mine is at the beginning of December so all in all there's just too much going on. I think I only ever truly relax on Christmas day night. Of course this is probably very similar for everyone and I think you don't actually really enjoy yourself at the time. I tend to look back and say "oh yes that was fun". I only seem to realise I had a good time afterwards. Of course Peter won't be here this year and I know Ben and I will find that hard. It will be strange when he's not around the dinner table with us and the kids. I wonder if we should go to a restaurant for Christmas dinner this year.

Wednesday.
Something came to me today. I'm not one for asking for advice or enquiring about other people's perspectives on things. I think I'm like this because I don't want to give anyone the chance to say something I don't

like. I hate negativity and I hate people been critical of me, it really affects me emotionally. But let me say this, it's only the people I like and love that upset me. Stranger's opinions mean nothing, and I mean nothing! But if someone I care for says something that is just plain nasty; I have great difficulty coping with it. I really don't understand those women who have to run everything they do past a dozen friends. If you don't know your own mind then you certainly won't when you have another twelve views on the issue.

Thursday.

I, lulu and penny went out to one of my favourite local pubs for lunch today. When I first asked lulu I think she thought it was a special occasion but I like to make time for myself just as I make time for my friends, children and family. When it was time to leave, penny pulled up after a job interview. We invited her along but I think she thought she was intruding. No way was she intruding, the more the merrier and I'm really not one to hog my friends and want them for myself. Anyway, we had a lovely meal, even if it did take two hours. Good god those women can talk. Lulu looked a bit bored at one point but I later found out that she's not very well.

Friday. Ben went with Noah on his school trip today and because Moses had a training day we both spent the day together doing the things he wanted to do. Both of my sons often ask if they can have a day with just me, one to one. I don't mind as I find they always behave a lot better when there on their own. Moses has taken a shine to embroidery and has made me promise not to tell his friends about it. We went down to the craft shop with my mum and picked up a few things for his new hobby and picked something up for lunch. It's been a quiet day but a relaxing one.

Saturday. I hate drinking. Ever since I started my Lithium my body has held up its judgmental hand and told the pinot gigot to piss off! But every now and then I'm just gagging for a drink of something strong and fruity, and I don't mean Ben. I love margarita and although I know it affects my medication I just couldn't help myself tonight. Alcohol helps me sleep and combined with my medication, I was out like a light. I know I know, how irresponsible.

Sunday. My mum must be psychic because she asked if we wanted to come for Christmas dinner this year. I don't think we've had Christmas dinner with her for ten years. My mum pointed out to me that because Peter wouldn't be there this year I could pretty much do what I wanted. I think it's going to be nice just been able to go to mums and not have a load of organising to do especially with the way my mood takes a nose drive at Christmas. I really should get round to asking her if we can bring our own meat, and potatoes and desert. I know that's cheeky but Ben and I are used to adding flavour to our food, whereas mum and dad turn their nose up at just the smallest amount of salt and pepper on the chicken skin. I mean they won't ever eat garlic. If I offer my dad garlic, any sauce or real gravy I am supplied with his one word stroke answer. MUCK!

Too much analysing.

Monday. After I dropped the kids a school this morning id decided I'd get a head start on the Christmas shopping. I know it seems early on the first day of October but the festive time of the year is a difficult one for me and I have to be as organised as possible to ensure I am fit for the celebrations and I'm able to make sure the kids have as much fun as possible. I asked Noah to do me a list of gifts he wanted and I have ordered a fair bit from EBay. I always wait until the end of November for Moses though as he changes his mind more than a menstrual fifty year old spinster. I really feel as though the old Emma has woken back up and joined the human race again. I've often asked the question "who am I?" but I think this opens me up to too much interpretation about myself and that's never good. I am who I am, good, bad, useless or just plain bloody marvellous. I can't change me so I may as well just love me.

Tuesday

well it's been quite a good day today. My car has only been on the auto trader for twenty minutes and someone called from London and will be coming up tomorrow for the car. I'm worried now that I'll be without a car, with Ben at university and me taking two kids to two different schools I'll be a little stuck. Anyway, Ben and I had a trip to a department outlet store today and he bought me a nice jumper and we had lunch together. I was encourage at the end of the school day today when Noah came out and started telling me all about his Ethics and Philosophy class. Noah has never told me anything about his school day and I was really proud and very smiley.

Wednesday

I only ever stop and assess my life and the state of it when something's going wrong. As it is at the moment, there's nothing much wrong with my life at all. All the things in it I can see and recognise to be good and healthy and positive. You see these things have always been there, I just haven't seen it through the eyes of a healthy woman. I'm getting there, I really am, I know so many people get sick because they just think, asses, compare and ostracize themselves far too much. I should be happy with that because I sure as hell am not going to analyse everything I do down to the smallest thing when I'm on my death bed. I want to be a wise old woman and you don't get that by been unless. We should be grateful, deal with the crap in our lives or we aren't able to rise above other people's silly nonsense. That's me, wise Emma.

Thursday.

I woke up this morning with a terrible headache and the only painkillers I had were co-codamol. These can be helpful but they blow up my belly like I'm about to drop a ten pound baby/ dump. The virgin television man wasn't supposed to come until twelve but decided to come at eight in the morning. Moses was been a horrible little cretin and I told him he wasn't going to his friends for dinner so he started to throw his book bag around. I didn't even get to say good bye to Noah and the man from London's coming for the car this afternoon. I'm not happy and I'm not feeling the calm serenity I should be feeling. Well the guy came for the car and he actually tried to bargain me down even more. Who the hell comes from London knowing I have already giving him my best price and tries to knock me down even further. Anyway the cheeky sod didn't get anywhere and if he didn't buy the car he would have had to pay at least one hundred pounds to get home. Silly man!

Friday. BOTOX DAYYYYYYYYY. I WILL BE BEAUTIFUL.

Why do people say, you don't need Botox. Well obviously I don't need it, because I've already had it! STUPID! I came home with six small bruises on my forehead, my face bled a little but apparently this is because I'm on a few different medications at the moment. I can't remember it hurting this much before but hey, it's got to be done.

Saturday.

I think I'm just letting Moses get away with his behaviour to have an easy life. I can't keep letting him get away with murder; it isn't fair to us or him. I try to be tougher but then I just feel bad. I'm at a loss.

Sunday.

Sunday dinner was a nonstarter today so we took the kids to the new Jamie Oliver restaurant for dinner. Wow it was expensive, for me anyway. One hundred and ten pounds! What was I thinking? I think that place will be reserved for special occasions.

Monday.

Taking Noah to school today was a nightmare. We only have one car at the moment and although that may sound a little greedy and ungrateful it's very necessary to have two when you have two children at too different school that can't make their own way to school. Ben dropped Moses off at 8:15 for breakfast club while I got a taxi at 8:20 with Noah. Although I had asked for the taxi to take me home again he told me he couldn't because he had a big job on so I would have to get out. I tried to call another taxi but there wasn't one for forty minutes. I decided to walk home and forty minutes later I arrived home soaked, knackered, in pain and dying for a wee.

Tuesday. Ben and I have been having quite a difficult time with Moses lately. I got a phone call from the deputy head who told me Moses had been screaming at his teaching assistant today and that he had been throwing things about in class and generally been unruly. She asked me if he had any problems at home, I told her the weekend had been hard and that all Moses was doing all the time was acting really ungrateful and been nasty to Noah. He just doesn't understand other peoples thinking. He has a huge lack of "theory of mind". I don't quite know what she wanted me to do but I agreed I would speak to him, and I did. I was determined to be really firm with him but when I saw him after school and saw how sad he was I mellowed slightly. He knew he was in trouble so I told him I got a call and I wasn't happy. I let him know that as soon as he starts been nasty to others I would take his things away. He then replied "can I have forty pound to buy world or war craft?" I just looked at him and said no, I'm sad with you. He was silent on the way home. One good thing today, Ben bought a new car so no more taxis and no more walking.

Wednesday.

Tonight is Moses high school open evening. I went with Noah last year so I've left this one up to Ben to "enjoy". I've bought a snuggly new pair of pyjamas and my back is giving me gip so I'm staying in front of the telly with Noah and may share a large bag of crisps with him. I've applied for Moses to go to the same school as Noah but as his behaviour has become increasingly difficult lately I'm going to look into the new autistic school on the other side of the city. The school is a free school and uses ABA Therapy for all students which concern's me a little but I'm certainly going to have a look round to see what they can offer.

Thursday.

Moses has decided to grow extra teeth from the top of his gums. He has beautiful teeth but this is not a pretty sight. I'm currently looking for a autism friendly dentist and good god are these hard to find. I can't exactly ask a dentist if he likes autistic people and they certainly don't advertise their likeness of the disorder on their websites. Help, my son can eat an apple threw a tennis racket!

Friday.

I have been the laziest mother/ wife/ mad head/ loony toon/ sexy love god from hell ever today. I dropped Noah at school, watched the wright stuff, prepared dinner, read my book for an hour, had a cuppa at my friend's house and even managed to fit in thirty minutes on the treadmill. I probably should have cleaned up but I'm not mother of the year so sod it! Ben and I are having a bottle of vino tonight so who knows what might happen. Wink wink.

Saturday.

I had a lot of hope for today but it started and ended in the exact same way, badly. At five thirty am Moses barged into Noah's bedroom and all hell let loose. Screaming, crying and throwing Nerf guns in the air. Moses just doesn't understand how his behaviour affects other people and gets very confused when I discipline him. I feel incredibly guilty taking his things away and making him sit on a chair in the middle of the kitchen but what kind of mother would I be if I didn't say what I mean and mean what I say? I have to make boundaries and I have to enforce rules. If I don't, I'm only letting my sons down and our whole family. My son is ten and if I don't start getting very tough ill lose his respect. I can't allow that.

Sunday.

I had to get the kids out of the house today, so I got there gear on and took them to the cinema while Ben started Sunday dinner and finished his Uni essay. I was really bored, Diary of a wimpy kid is really not my thing but the kids were pretty well behaved and I ate lots of crap so we all left happy.

Monday.

Ben has been at Uni all day today so I've had a lot of time on my hands to get things done. Noah has an appointment to see a specialist tomorrow regarding the possibility of brain damage. It's worrying me, not because I'm scared of there been anything wrong because he will always be perfect to me, but rather that I don't want my concerns to be just dismissed. This has happened on so many occasions and I find I go into mental mother on a mission mode. Which is affective but not pretty?

Tuesday.

Ben and I picked Noah up at one and took him to the specialist he was due to see. Dr Robinson was lovely and we all felt quite at ease with her. She was enthusiastic and listened to our concerns. After an hour Noah got a bit upset because he was really bored and just wanted to incessantly talk about transformers and Moses bad behaviour. I spoke to the doctor on my own for a while and she advised me on therapists, key workers to help Noah with his independence and a blood test that could help us determine which side of the family the Autism probably came from. I didn't think the test was constructive or helpful so I declined it. Overall she was quite informative and even gave me the number of a good dentist close by for both the kids.

Wednesday.

Homework, homework, homework, it's just not natural or healthy to send a eleven year old home with nine pieces of homework in one week. Overall it's me putting the effort in. Of course Noah is doing the homework but I'm the one who has to make sure he doesn't miss any and I'm the one who has to sit at the computer with him for four hours doing a PowerPoint presentation with him on the five generations of our family. Who's the pupil here?

Thursday.

Noah seems to be coming home very positive and enthusiastic recently. He's really beginning to enjoy school although he would deny it if I asked him. For dinner tonight I made homemade burgers with lamb mince from the butchers with sundried tomatoes and feta cheese in the middle. I did plain ones for the kids but they went down quite well.

Friday.
A famous author visited Moses school today and told the kids all about Mokey Joe. Moses came home so animated and insisted on buying one of the books from Amazon. We jumped on the computer and ordered his favourite one and I was relieved to see it was only a few pounds. I asked him all about the books and became really excited and became very theatrical and energetic. I smiled; this is my Moses, happy Moses.

Saturday.
I think the weight loss from losing Peter has finally come to a halt and has transformed into a massive u turn. I've put on half a stone in three weeks. Maybe I'm finally becoming more content. But sod content if content = fat!

Sunday.
Ben and Moses went shooting clays today with our friends so I decided Noah and I would spend a little time together. How wrong was I? All Noah wanted to do was play with his transformers and although I tried to engage in his game it was difficult to really interact when his whole thought process was transformer related. He was in his own world, filled with angry Auto bots and menacing

deceptacons. I let him get on with it as I think I was spoiling his fun.

Monday.
Last night I went to the pub with three friends' I've known for years. When we arrived at the pub I noticed a lady id made friends with recently at Noah's new school. She was sat with her husband and called us all over. She's a nice woman but I always feel like she trying to get information out of me and I find it a bit uncomfortable. She has one of those tones in her voice that comes across as gossipy and nosey and that everything she says seems to come across as a salacious piece of gossip, when it's really not. Anyway, we had a good evening but that night she text me and told me that she thought my friend was really irritating and did I agree that she was a know it all. I got really annoyed. This is coming from some board housewife, gossip that has never worked a day in her life! My friend is a psychiatrist, foster parent and Krav Maga instructor. The thing that really upset me was the fact that she thought it was ok to be rude about a woman she knew nothing about. I don't slag off my friends so I decided to ignore her, and the next four texts.

Tuesday.
My car has started to rattle so I put it in for a check-up and ended up with a bill of over two hundred pounds. I had to lend the cash from my mum as I didn't just have that amount of disposable cash. After a trip to the supermarket I came home and read up on some autism research that the doctor had given me yesterday. Overall, a rather dull, but functional day. Whatever the hell that means!

Wednesday.
My Botox bruises are finally going and in a couple of day I'm sure I would have lost the "battered errant wife" look. Every now and then I seem to get obsessed with the way I look and can't stop looking in mirrors, exfoliating, mudpacks and new makeup purchased. I'm in that phase right now but I seem to be concentrating far too much on looking in the mirror in my car while I'm driving. I hate my teeth, my hair is thin and brittle and my skin is uneven, and don't even get me started on my fat arse and saggy belly. I'm off to Tenerife in February with the family and I am determined to be slim and toned. The diet starts now! Well it's three in the afternoon so better start tomorrow.

Thursday.

I forced myself almost kicking and screaming to the gym today, I have to give myself motivation so I bought one of those trashy brain-dead magazines and cut out loads of pictures of slim looking women and put them on the fridge, nest to my bead and in the study. I know this seems a bit silly but it works for me. My mum is giving up smoking and I'm really proud of her, she has never attempted to give up and it the ripe old age of fifty two she's trying. Lots of people in my family have or are giving up and Peter passing away has been a catalyst for a lot of people I know. I've never smoked, but I guess it's the same as anything in that if you don't want to quit then you won't. Both my mum and dad smoke and there both quite heavy drinkers. One of my brothers is a heavy drinker and they both smoke. I'm neither and I don't know if that's because I left home at sixteen and they had less of an influence on me. I just got the mental case gene.

Friday.

I've been really argumentative, irritable and moody around people today and it's getting a little out of control. All I seem to do is raise my voice and scream on my own in the back garden. My neighbours will think I'm crazy screaming arse, bollocks bum fun fucker ten at night.

Everyone who works in customer service irritates me and I deliberately pick arguments with them. I think customer service, be it banks, restaurants or the orange women on the Chanel counter who look like they've shagged a Wotsit is just terrible in this country. It's a rarity that staff go above and beyond their basic duties. I once went to have my eyes tested at vision express and I was suffering for postnatal depression and hadn't left the house for three weeks. Ben called the optician and explained this but when I got there the woman was just rude. She spoke to me like a second class citizen and informed me I shouldn't be having my eyes tested if I was in such a state as I was obviously wasting her time with my dramatic tears. I was mortified.

Saturday.

I spoke to Ben last night while I was doing the ironing and we wrote a whole planned list for the weekend. We decided on Nostel Priory for Saturday with Chinese buffet for dinner and Harwood house for Sunday followed by fish and chips in front of the television. Normal family shit really. I wonder why I feel the need to plan everything.

Sunday.

Every couple of weeks I make a point of visiting my grandmother who lives in the next town. I also usually pop into see my great grandmother who lives a few doors down. Anyway I stopped off at Sainsbury's and bought two bouquets of flowers for them both as I know they both really love flowers. I had a cup of tea at my grans and we chatted about the most recent books we were reading and the gossip on of my grandfather's gout and then set off to my great grandma's house. When I got there my gran was at her other daughter's house but I was met by my mother who had been doing the cleaning. I put the flowers in a vase and took my mother to the "top shops" so she could go to the sunbeds. I could tell my mum that the sunbeds will be the death of her but what's the point. Who am I to tell a grown woman what she already knows? She has to do it alone.

Monday.

I went to the doctors this morning. I've been having trouble getting up on a morning and bursting into tears for no reason. If someone would ask me what the matter was I would just say nothing. And that's the truth, I am fine, my life is fine. The doctor game me a week's course of diazepam as people with bipolar can't take antidepressants, not that I think feeling weepy and down merits them anyway. Diazepam wasn't what I was expecting but I'll take them as and when I feel I need them and see how it goes.

Tuesday.
Good god I am tired. So now I am in tears, and exhausted. I've been sleeping most of the day and only got up to do the ironing and read the kids a bedroom story. At ten tonight I felt Moses climb into bed with me and he read six pages of his book bone breaker to me, after we agreed on one. There's something so comforting about your little one snuggling up to you if a big cosy bed. I slept happy and content that night and even more happily when Ben joined me and cuddled me until I told him to get off as he was making me hot. Who sleeps cuddling all night? That's just bloody weird.

Wednesday.
I woke up this morning feeling terrible. It seems that whenever I have a little bit of physical illness my mood takes a whack too. I took Noah to school and stopped off at the local garage. I like the garage because it sells marked down food all day long. I bought a large flapjack, two packets of crisps, a bacon sandwich and a pastry, all costing one pound forty. I drove the few minutes it takes to get home

and went back to bed and ate the lot while watching crappy television. At one in the afternoon Ben opened the door and pulled the chain clean off. I couldn't believe id been asleep for so long. I'm putting weight on and it's really worrying me, I'd done so well losing so much but I have to be in the right mind set to do it. God it's hard, especially when you feel so run down.

Thursday.
I hope this illness doesn't last for much longer. I've been having a lot of thoughts about Halloween recently. I love that time of year and I always decorate the front of the house but this year I'm going way over the top. There is a narrow path leading down my drive and I want to create a kind of hovel and a small outside cave filled with dry ice and caldrons. There's nothing like scaring the shit out of kids to make you piss yourself with laughter. I swear to god I'll go to hell.

Friday.
Today I found a film on picture box called Adam. I read the info and it said it was about a man with Asperger's syndrome. Usually I shy away from there types of film as they make me sad but after watching the trailer and reading the feedback I decided I would watch it. I sat in my living room with the sun glaring in feeling

rather positive. I often want to climb into Noah's brain if just for a second, just see if he's happy. That's my life goal, to make my boys happy and content. The job, money or a fast car mean nothing. Just happiness, that's all I want. I suppose that's what most parents want. The film gave me hope, not that I didn't have it anyway but it's nice now and then have find a positive perspective on the condition. I got that warm feeling in my belly that brought a smile to my face. Adam finds a woman, a patient woman who wants to know more about his condition. It made me feel good and my day was brighter. I smiled so many times throughout the film, you know moments I could relate too? Sometimes feeling sad one minute and happy the next about a subject close to your heart makes you feel like you've done something that needed doing.

Saturday.

At the end of this week Noah has had sixteen pieces of homework. This really isn't right. For a start it's me who has to organise him doing this homework as he doesn't have the same cogs moving in his brain as other children to motivate himself. This isn't just a matter of pushing him; his memory to complete the homework isn't relevant when he leaves the classroom. On top of this Moses has spellings, learning log and maths homework. Kids, especially at high school have way too much pressure on them. Although in Noah's case the pressure is on me.

Sunday.

I'm absolutely penniless and I really need to rein back my spending so I have promised myself any money spent up until next Tuesday will only be spent on food and petrol. Having a two litre engine really isn't helping my finances so ill only have to go out when I need to get the kids. I've bought lots of Christmas present recently so that makes me feel a little better as I always start to panic at this time of year. I hate it when my routine changes and this always happens at the festive end of the year. Ben suggested we go to my favourite restaurant for my birthday with four of our friends this year and to be honest I really can't wait, it will be simple, not much organising and a simple relaxed evening in great company.

Monday.

I attended an autism group in my local town today. I hated it. It wasn't about the kids at all it was a bunch of uneducated layabouts moaning about benefits and how there screaming kids wouldn't do what they said. Newsflash ladies, autistic people have problems understanding other people and fitting into society like the rest of us take for granted and let's be honest if they don't even understand their teachers there sure as hell not going to understand the likes of Mr and Mrs Dumbass as parents. Oh and having children with disabilities does not equal a fat benefit cheque at the end of the month. Get a job, get an education and for Christ's sake get some sure deodorant. I can't see me going back there again.

The future is bright............because I bloody said so!

So here I am. A year on from the advice I was given by a dear friend to write down all my honest thoughts a feelings in an attempt to rid them from my over loaded brain. In many ways it's worked and in others it's been a little torturous. Over the last year Ben and I have been tested, struggled and found happiness in the strangest of places but what's for sure, we have dealt with all that has been thrown at us like the strong family unit we are. I worry and will always worry about my sons and there development but I know that together Ben and I will encourage their mental wellbeing and help them grow into happy young men who enjoy even the smallest of wonders. As for me, I continue to struggle with who I am, my temper, my tactless ways and sometimes blatant rudeness but I know in some way my health is improving and certainly has since this time last year. So here's to the next twelve months.

Happiness really isn't a destination. It's a way of life. Live for now.

Miss you harry.

To protect the privacy of certain individuals the names and identifying details have been changed.

Back page

If you're looking for some life changing piece of literature that's going to make you the world's best parent of an autistic child then put this book down. It's honest. It will make you laugh and cry and it will show you real life with light at the end of the tunnel. Parents like us always need a little honesty; not like what we get from those "professionals"

By E J Plows.

Made in the USA
Monee, IL
08 September 2020

41688422R00125